The Uneducated English

The Uneducated English.

WINIFRED M. WHITELEY

METHUEN & CO LTD
11 New Fetter Lane · London EC4

First published 1969 by Methuen & Co Ltd
11 New Fetter Lane, London EC4
© 1969 by Winifred M. Whiteley
Printed in Great Britain by
Ebenezer Baylis and Son, Ltd.
The Trinity Press, Worcester and London

Distributed in the U.S.A. by Barnes & Noble Inc.

Contents

Acknowledgements   *page* vii

  I The Aims of this Book   1
 II Living in an Urban Environment   5
III Basic Intellectual Training   25
 IV Widening the Range of Aesthetic Experience   38
  V Moral Training   51
 VI The Changing Role of Women and its
     Educational Implications   66
VII Coloured Immigrants in Schools   79
VIII Educational Selection: Comprehensives and
     Streaming   104
 IX Teachers   150
  X In Conclusion   171

     Reading List   177

     Index   181

Acknowledgements

I have received help and information from so many Heads and staffs of schools that it would be impossible to list everyone. In particular I would like to acknowledge indebtedness to Mrs Peggy Bamfield, Mr Basil Noble, Mr Sidney Morris of the Birmingham University School of Education, and Mr T. G. Ayre, formerly Welfare Liaison Officer to the Commonwealth Council for the West Midlands who supplied information on coloured immigrants. I would also like to thank my husband, Dr Charles Whiteley, of the Philosophy Department of Birmingham University, for all the encouragement he has given me in my first venture as an independent author, and for his invaluable help with the organization of my material.

I · The Aims of this Book

In writing this book I have had two main purposes. The first was to provide a sequel to *The Permissive Morality*, which my husband and I published in 1964. That was a book in which we examined changes that have taken place during the present century in British moral attitudes, and suggested a complex of economic and intellectual causes for them. We observed a steady movement away from the old rule-bound morality of Victorian times towards a more permissive utilitarian morality which seeks the promotion of happiness. Each style of morality has its own advantages and defects. The typical defect of the new permissive morality is that it tends to promote a couldn't-care-less attitude among those who miss the pressures of the stricter code. In discussing our views with all kinds of people we found considerable agreement with us on this point, and it was often said that education should do more towards getting young people to care about values and standards. When we asked just what it was that education was supposed to do nobody had a clear answer. Yet a clear answer is very much needed, as magistrates, probation officers, youth leaders and others who have to do with the young know only too well. Anyone who reads Michael Schofield's *Sexual Behaviour of Young People* will be struck by the note of uncertainty that sounds throughout their comments on sex morality. Even more striking is the absence of any sort of conviction about what would make life worth while on the part of the teenagers encountered by Mary Morse's social workers among *The Unattached*. Among the many books on our adolescents that have appeared during the past few years, these two especially reveal drifting where there should be personal aspirations and commitments. It is impossible to read such books without wondering how these youngsters were taught during their ten or more years in school. Scarcely anything seems to have stuck that might have enabled them to find significance in their own lives either at work or during leisure. This is not solely a feature of working-class or secondary-modern society, for the 'Seagate' group were largely middle-class, some of them ex-grammar school pupils. Similarly Professor Musgrove, in *Family, Education and Society*, found large numbers of pupils expressing dissatisfaction with their grammar schools in respect of their own expectations from them of emotional security, freedom, friendship, sense of competence, support from adults, identity with a group and sense of purpose. It looks as though the delinquent group may be only the visible tip of an iceberg consisting of all those who are not living up to capacity, people who are perfectly capable of doing and appreciating far more than they do but in fact pass their lives at an idling pace.

So I am prompted to ask these questions: Are we even now doing all that we could in our schools to provide children with a lead in to the numerous patterns of living which *can* give satisfaction under the conditions of today? Are we managing to demonstrate to them why life without standards is a mess? Are we taking enough account of the many pressures of our urbanized society, so that we can equip the young to stand up to them? Is the basic intellectual training good enough – the training, not only in literacy and numeracy, but in the making of inferences in everyday situations, and in the art of fixing one's attention on its object and maintaining it undistracted? Why do we not try to give them more insight into their own personal relationships, which for almost half the school population, the girls, are the most important thing in life? Couldn't we induce them to think more about the consequences of whatever they do? And why do we make the mistake of assuming that aesthetic experience is confined to enjoyment of the 'arty', which working-class youngsters commonly believe to be effeminate? What are we doing to prepare this generation for the changes in the roles of men and women, for increasing geographical mobility of the people at large, and for the social integration of white and coloured in our society? All these questions raise issues which need to be tackled at once if young people are to be helped to mature instead of merely being bored in school. This does not involve further burdensome additions to overweighted curricula so much as a change in the attitude of many teachers to their work, so that the teaching relevant to the issues can be incorporated within the framework of what is already being done.

My second objective was to examine the organization of our schools (tripartite or comprehensive, streamed or unstreamed) and the selection, training and deployment of teachers, including heads, to see whether these are well adapted to the aims I am suggesting for education. There is, so far as I know, no Handbook for Head Teachers, nor any specific form of training for their work (the same applies to deputy head teachers). We fuss about the employment of graduates without teaching diplomas in our schools, yet apparently nobody sees anything wrong with turning a man (or woman) into the sole arbiter of a school's policies without first giving him a thorough briefing on his duties, the problems he will have to solve, and the general purposes of education itself. There are indeed some wonderful head teachers, but preliminary training should provide us with a good many more. I have also asked whether training institutions are realistic enough in their approach to would-be teachers, whether they prepare them adequately for the difficulties they are bound to meet in some classrooms, whether they draw sufficiently on the experience of those who have successfully taught big classes, unruly classes, and classes in which a third or more of the children are coloured and as yet unused to our way of life. And I draw attention to the ills attending our rat-race system of promotion, especially the high rate of teacher turnover that it brings about.

Throughout the book I have borne in mind the question I first raised in *The Permissive Morality*, namely, how can we best help people to live satisfying lives in our urban mass society? Somehow in school we have to persuade youngsters to make the best of things instead of the worst. I have begun to see that herein lies the basic difference between the general attitude to life prevailing during my own teens and that which prevails today. People really used to try to make the best of it; but nowadays far too many do nothing of the sort. It may be too late to modify the outlook of most adults, but in our schools we have the experience of the future in the making. We must do everything conceivable to ensure that that experience will turn out to have been for everyone 'a life worth living'.

In the course of preparing this book I have read dozens by other people, some of which I recommend in my list of relevant reading matter. These are the books which in my opinion no trainee teacher should miss. Certain of them show that the profession has its darker side, but so has every other profession. I have also visited a number of schools, whose head teachers and staff showed me a good deal of what was going on in their classrooms and answered my batteries of questions with noteworthy patience and good-humour. I should like to testify to the enthusiasm of many of those I met.

II · Living in an Urban Environment

From the beginning I want to make it plain that my account of the effects which English urbanized society can be expected to have on young people is not a series of inferences from statistics obtained in research. It is to a considerable extent impressionistic, describing the pressures of our society as many of us see and feel them. To establish beyond doubt the connections I wish to suggest between the features to which I draw attention and the boredom and restlessness of some of our young people would require a vast amount of research. Yet if we must await the results of such research before acknowledging the more unfortunate effects of urbanized society in the young, then we shall lose valuable time that could be used in getting to grips with the problems. I believe that ordinary observation and inference can show us many ways in which their environment is harmful to people of all age groups, but it is in our schools that we have the best opportunities of equipping them to lead satisfying lives that are not anti-social, despite the frustrations and difficulties of life in many English towns today.

Most people have been impressed with the effects of increasingly rapid technical and social change.[1] Ever since the beginning of the Industrial Revolution the pace of technical change has become steadily greater. It affects everyone at almost every moment of his life, at work or at leisure. As scientists extend their enquiries some problems are mastered. But the developments to which the solutions themselves give rise occasion further problems. Thus over the past sixty years or so, people alive today have seen the techniques of warfare, transport, communications, building, heating, food conservation and marketing completely transformed. These transformations have combined with an increase in population to bring us to the verge of world shortages in land, water, food and fuel. They have also caused massive pollution of air and water and

[1] Since I wrote the above, the Schools Council has published its Working Paper 12; *Implications of Social and Economic Change*.

5

a formidable amount of noise. Attempts to deal with the shortages and to lessen noise and pollution will inevitably bring about still further changes in techniques. The outcome of this is that the living conditions, the work, and the day to day problems of people in all civilized countries change ever more rapidly from year to year. This rate of change can be expected to go on accelerating.

In time not merely a few but perhaps the majority of the working population will be faced with complete retraining for some other sort of work. Others will need to take refresher courses on newer methods of doing their jobs. To cope with such experiences people will need to remain mentally flexible until they are past early middle age. It seems possible that three types of worker will be in demand. The first type will be well drilled operatives of lowish skill but capable of long spells of repetitive activity, for despite the advance of automation it is unlikely that repetition jobs will quickly disappear from the industrial scene. But many of these low-skilled workers will probably find that in order to remain employed they must be prepared to move from job to job and even from place to place, somewhat like spare parts. They must be able to fit in anywhere, industrially and socially. The financial rewards of this role can be considerable. Such a worker need not be very clever so long as he has nimbleness of fingers or other physical knacks and a steady work rhythm, but he must be ready for a change of task. He must be brought up on the idea that we live in a changing world and must change with it, and that in most jobs a certain docility is essential. Inevitably the more important part of his life is going to be his leisure, from which he should be equipped to get every possible satisfaction.

A second type of worker, who with advancing automation may well become far commoner, is the service hand, whose skills will vary from the relatively low level of shop assistant or bus conductor to the higher levels of the electrical maintenance man, or the garage mechanic. Service work thus employs many grades of intelligence yet all of it requires watchfulness and readiness to respond to demand. Thus there is an important personality difference between the service hand and other kinds of worker. If we classify teachers, nurses and doctors among service workers as I think we should, this point will become clearer. No young person who does not genuinely feel impelled to help others should be encouraged to prepare for a career in any sort of service work, yet at the present day too many of them are cynically lacking in this basic requirement.

The third type of worker is necessarily intelligent and highly trained: the discoverer, inventor, designer or organiser. Such people are not interchangeable like the relatively unskilled, yet nevertheless they similarly face changes of living place because promotion is usually to a job in some other town. By contrast most service workers can rely on staying as long as they choose in some one place.

But as we consider the future lives of all workers we are forced to concede that everyone has to be adaptable and ready for change, either of working technique or of living place if not of both. Young people now face a life in which the one who is most on his toes is at a great advantage. It is a forward looking society in which the past no longer counts for very much except to the sentimental and the elderly. Looking back at the older people I knew as a girl I am astonished to realize how very much stuck in a rut most of them were. They used to live thirty years or more in the same house, still furnished with things they had installed there when they got married. The sideboard had sometimes come from a great aunt and there might be ornaments dating back a hundred years. People kept favourite old clothes, old walking sticks, old books that they never opened . . . the roomier cupboards of those days encouraged hoarding. Current fashion did not unduly disturb their arrangements, nor did they budge far from the routines they had evolved long since. Before most people had cars the annual holiday, if they went away at all, was often to the same resort year after year. A static way of life, and perhaps not a little boring. But the people who lived it knew what to expect from year to year, barring accident, serious illness or unemployment. They did not need sedatives so much as 'a nice change' and the smallest divergence from normal routine was enough to give that. When we comment on the restlessness and rootlessness of life today perhaps we ought to recall more clearly what the old settled existence was actually like . . . boring, frustrating, a life wherein gossip occupied a good part of the role that television does today. Somewhere between these extremes we have to help young people to find a style of adjustment to life in which change can be digested comfortably because they have developed within themselves a serene centre.

It is beginning to be suspected that people are more affected than they realize by the pressures of urban environment. Shortage of physical space is increasingly noticeable in our larger towns. The home of today, whether house, flat or rented rooms, is for many very cramped and cramping. Newly built rooms are often no larger than those in houses which today are thought only fit to be pulled down. The recently built dwelling may only have modern heating and sanitation to commend it. Instances of new privately built houses in Stroud, Gloucestershire, include:

Example One. First bedroom, 100 sq ft, second bedroom, 97½ sq ft, third bedroom, 75 sq ft. From which we may infer a total area on both floors of little more than 545 sq ft.

But the ceiling of 1,000 sq ft put on the areas of new houses after the war was then regarded as restrictive!

Example Two. First bedroom, 126 sq ft, second bedroom, 108 sq ft, third bedroom, 50 sq ft. From which we may infer a total area of little more than 568 sq ft.

At the Annual Conference of the Urban District Councils Association at Paignton in June 1967, Councillor Thomas Cameron in a paper on space in new houses quoted the above figures and added that in a recent housing scheme submitted to his council the kitchen of the houses had a total area of 45 sq ft, and that after installation of fittings the free area in the middle of the room measured only 3 ft 6 in by 2 ft 9 in, although under the provisions of the Housing Act of 1957 a room of less than 50 sq ft is not considered to be a habitable room. A planning department official of Birmingham City Council said that they too had a number of applications where the room sizes were not up to the standards of the Act, often with tiny kitchens full of doors so that it would be difficult even to instal fittings and furniture. It is interesting to compare the measurements of the houses being privately built in Stroud with the recommended minimum standards of local authority housing published by the Ministry of Housing and Local Government in 1952. These are:

First bedroom, 135 sq ft, second bedroom, 110 sq ft, third bedroom, 70 sq ft, living-dining room, 225 sq ft, kitchen, 90 sq ft. Total area, 630 sq ft, exclusive of bathroom and passageways.

Today's privately built houses are smaller than what was already in 1952 a minimal standard for local authority housing. The government may be urged to intervene but already there are great numbers of these over-compact homes.

We try to counter this tendency by making chairs and tables smaller and throwing out the piano. Another common expedient is to do away with partitioning walls on the ground floor, giving the open plan house in which entrance hall, dining room and sitting room form a single unit and only the kitchen is separate. In some districts however (e.g. Nantwich, to judge by house specifications in house agents' windows) the kitchen is more usually in one with the dining room, leaving a separate sitting room. But as many have learned with dismay, open plan means an end to privacy for purposes of study, courting or separating those members of the household who want to watch or listen to different programmes or records at the same time. We cannot consign the courting couples to the bedrooms nor exclude children from the only living room. Not much hope of gracious living here. Bitter rows arise between devotees of different television programmes and some homes become little hells, as any teacher who visits parents of children with problems can testify. So, at a time when the advertisers assure us that the world is our oyster, daily life can easily become less satisfactory. Hobbies cannot be pursued without room to spread out their materials and to store them when not in use. People are forced either to go out or to sit in front of the dominating television screen, which has the merit of keeping several people in a small area quiet and still for hours on end. At the same time it provides the perfect escape from that constricting little room into the scenes that it calls up. In the too-small living room of today we see an environment which cramps people physically and mentally, and prevents them from pursuing their interests in a creative manner at home, thus fostering (one may suspect) a shut-in feeling which they can most easily relieve by projecting themselves into the places and personalities of the television world. The 'box' is the perfect, the essential object to put into the modern living room because its use makes little call on physical space but instead provides an impression of endless space on call, together with an unending supply of vicarious experiences to fill out the lives starved of direct experience of their own. Before the war *the* escapist outlet was the cinema, which did at least compel its addicts to get out of the house, usually on foot, to visit it, and supplied a big screen on which fine photography could be seen in telling detail. It is in keeping with our overcrowded age that the principal entertainment screen should have shrunk along with other space-occupying things (except of course motor cars). The perfect escapist device from every point of view is a book. But to many, reading will seem hard work in comparison with lounging in front of the 'box' and looking on.

From the dwelling let us pass to its immediate surroundings. It is unusual for flats to have private gardens, and no houses built of late have more than enough space to hang the washing, and for a few persons to sit out of doors. They certainly are not gardens in which children can play at cops and robbers. No more were ours when I was young. But *we* had as supplement the streets and tunnelled side entries of terraced housing. We could play there even on the surface of the roadway itself, where we chalked hop-scotch plots and used long skipping ropes. Our great delight was long games of hide and seek spread over several blocks of housing. We felt free to come and go, independent of transport . . . a feeling I find lacking in many town children now. The reasons for this change are obvious enough: first the traffic which makes street play dangerous and determines many mothers to keep their off-spring within sight, usually in some small enclosure; and secondly, sidewalks already used for parking cars and therefore no good for games with balls. Even walking in the streets as a pastime is a riskier and less pleasant experience than it used to be. Our children have lost the streets as an extension to home and backyard. The Parks? There they may meet with a gang of roughs who will break or steal their toys and bully them; such incidents have been described by indignant parents in letters to the *Birmingham Mail* during July 1967. Another risk for children on their own in the park is the sexual pervert, maybe no more common now than during my own childhood, but given so much publicity that prudent parents make him another reason for keeping children at home.

Cramped dwellings, small gardens or none, loss of freedom to run the streets and parks, and on holiday, the crowded beach where there is barely room to spread another towel, and sometimes caravan accommodation even more exiguous than that of home ... where then are our children to find freedom to run wild? The one remaining place seems to be school itself and its playground and sports fields. This is an important reason for not scanting the allocation of land to educational premises. Through them the cramped private dwelling can be supplemented by publicly owned space, especially if the school serves as a community centre for its catchment area.

We have not the climate for all-the-year-round pavement cafés, and our housing developments tend to lack the counterpart of the Italian piazza as it used to be before the Italians themselves spoiled it by parking cars all over it. (Venetian children are to be envied their traffic free squares where urchins play at cops and robbers as soon as they are let out of school.) But we could do more to foster street life even here, as it was in the 1920s before it was killed by broadcasting, wartime blackouts, and the family car, and people used to stroll along the roads and gaze in shopwindows in the evenings, to get a breath of air as they said. Perhaps in time our doctors will convince us that it really is unhealthy never to walk anywhere.

Meanwhile it is now largely the school and its grounds that must provide open space for our children, and perhaps the use of parks by organized play-groups. Unfortunately many town schools, especially in the inner ring, have crowded classrooms and play-grounds that have been encroached on for necessary additional building.

Anyone who doubts whether children really suffer from the situation to which I have drawn attention should watch them at play in the too-small playground and witness the collisions between boisterous youngsters with nowhere else to let off steam. West Indian children, who in their country of origin lived all day out of doors often upset their English teachers by pushing and knocking others down in corridors or playgrounds; they commonly come from families living in a single room or two rooms. It would be interesting to see any records of playground accidents, on which had been noted the home circumstances of the children involved, such as how many rooms they lived in and of what size, whether there was a private yard or garden, whether they habitually played in the streets or in a park. Nor would it be surprising to discover that children from a cramped environment were abnormally restless in the classroom.

The alternative is that they may become underexercised and flabby, easily tiring when required to exert themselves physically, and if overfed with sweets and cakes, then also unduly fat. Can the recent high rate of obesity among schoolchildren be entirely attributed either to glandular unbalance or too much carbohydrate in their diet? One would like to know how often the overfeeding is associated with life in a small dwelling and lack of spontaneous physical movement. A further risk to obese children is that when treated with amphetamine drugs to suppress their appetite, they may become addicted to these drugs. Dr Norman Imlah, the Medical Director of All Saints Hospital Birmingham, where studies of drug addiction are being made, publicly stated in the *Birmingham Mail* of July 11th, 1967 that these drugs 'are wrecking the lives of thousands of Midland boys and girls . . . Among addicts are some who end in mental hospitals when all that was originally wrong with them was that they were fat.' Rather an alarming sidelight on a situation which in turn may be demonstrably the outcome of housing families in flats or other small dwellings without gardens, in areas where street play is unsafe on account of traffic. The children may reach school at five unused to movement as a means to self-expression, heavy and gawky in games or dancing. An over-anxious mother who wants at all costs to keep them safe can be an additional factor in aggravating the situation, for she will have prevented them from jumping and running on the stairs of the flats or otherwise risking the usual childish tumbles. They grow up unwilling to attempt skating, mountain walking, or even any violent form of dancing; looseness of movement is unknown to them, they seldom make more than the feeblest of bodily efforts and no teacher can force them to do more. The outcome of this line of argument seems to be that nursery schools with spacious premises are vitally needed for all children whose home environment is cramping, not merely those from poor homes, since there is lack of space in many a relatively prosperous household. As soon as they can walk unaided children need play space in which to develop freely their powers of movement, with swings and climbing frames, preferably with supervision as well. Physical self confidence will never even begin without room for activity and if it is absent from home life and mothers cannot or will not take their children to the park, the nursery school is needed to take over.

A second effect of cramped living about which there can be no doubt is that where the home lacks storage space and somewhere to spread out work in progress, children will be unable to benefit fully from school instruction by going on with their craft work in their own homes. This may be why so little of the craft activity enjoyed in school is carried over into adult life; the average dwelling of today has nowhere to house it. Could not Evening Institutes provide lockers, and practice rooms where members could continue the work begun in class?

A third effect of urban overcrowding is the blatant lack of privacy. In the typical street of open plan housing passers-by habitually glance into each living room as they go along . . . and there is not a corner of the ground floor apart from the kitchen where the occupants are out of sight. They may be equally within the visual field of their neighbours in four or more houses across the street. It is like living in a goldfish bowl. Picture windows (often undraped) and lack of screening hedges, between them make the sense of exposure as complete as it can be. The normal reaction to this situation appears to be a defiant exhibitionism. In Holland, where the situation has prevailed even longer, the inhabitants of such houses leave their curtains undrawn at night so that the family are seen staging a show of their way of life, their belongings, their visitors, all that is theirs. This is in marked contrast with the former English working class habit of excluding prying eyes and everyone save members of the extended family. Today we are told desire for privacy is a middle class trait and its indulgence a luxury, or even faintly suspect. What has arisen is an extraordinary state of affairs in which few people are genuinely gregarious in the sense of regularly spending their leisure with friends, but the segregated nuclear family life is carried on in glass-sided boxes. It would surely be odd if this practice had no psychological effects whatever. Its exponents are not just unconcernedly leading their own lives in public (as West Indians do in the open air in their country of origin), they are almost incessantly exhibited with the enhancing effect of the picture window as frame, illuminated at night. No doubt the activity which gives away least of private feeling in these circumstances is watching television. So long as people do nothing but this and eating in their living rooms, nobody is any the wiser about their true interests. It is only a step farther to having no individual interests save those which are pursued in the bedroom! Is this really an advance on those stuffy little Edwardian family interiors? At least there was privacy there for indulging strong emotion behind the lace curtains and potted plants. Many today are forced by lack of privacy to become either conformists or exhibitionists. This might be one of the many factors contributing to the marked loss of spontaneity that teachers have noticed in children as they move into the secondary stage of schooling; maybe they have begun to realize that they are penned in and never without an audience. Again, as people begin to live packed ever closer together, may they not like laboratory rats show signs of pent-in frustration and impatience, which could eventually issue in vandalism?[1]

Perhaps we should be setting on foot research into the behaviour of contrasted groups of children from cramped environments and from homes with bigger rooms and gardens, or who simply enjoy regular street play or visits to the park. We might expect to see in the first group marked tendencies either towards lack of exercise and flabbiness or else to restlessness and accident-proneness. Do those who keep up their interest in school work tend to come from the roomier surroundings? Mary Morse in *The Unattached* points out that those bored and drifting young people 'were particularly affected by the overcrowded conditions in which they

---

[1] Vance Packard in *The Naked Society* describes effects of lack of privacy in the home due to thin partitions and open plan. A Dallas builder who advertised the 'Quiet House' got 3,400 visitors in one week-end – the largest turn-out he had seen in years. Packard maintains that lack of domestic privacy drives teenagers into gangs.

were living' . . . and 'in Northtown the lack of privacy, the frictions and the irritations caused by overcrowding seem to have added tensions to families which already suffered more than enough', so that these youngsters took to the streets.[1]

But overcrowding is far from being the only source of painful pressure on people in urbanized society. Most are sensitive to noise in varying degrees (whether they realize it or not, the effort of excluding it from attention tires them), and this country is rapidly becoming noisier. Road traffic here steadily increases, and in their efforts to avoid jams motorists now use side roads through residential areas so that traffic noise is spread throughout districts formerly free of it. To find a quiet bedroom on holiday taxes the ingenuity of anyone who wants to stay in a seaside resort, and the less said about hotel bedrooms in London the better. To surface traffic noise we must add the growing din of air traffic, especially trying to those who live below the flight paths of planes approaching or leaving airports. We are now in addition threatened with the nerve-racking sound of aircraft 'breaking the sound-barrier'. At night these could be guaranteed to wreck repose for those poor sleepers who lack confidence in their own ability to get off again. The interested parties, makers and operators of aircraft, form a powerful pressure group insisting to the government that there must be technical progress, cost what it may in terms of human well-being. They insinuate that the public will get used to anything. It is known that beyond a certain level of measurable noise there is damage to the eardrums. But so far nobody seems to have devised a means of measuring the nervous wear and tear, which may be at least as important as damage to eardrums since it impoverishes the quality of daily life: people who do not get enough sleep, and whose vitality is even further impaired by the effort of cutting out unwanted noise by day, are at a disadvantage as compared with those living in quieter surroundings. Yet so far there has been no serious move towards lessening the noisiness of any form of traffic, and it is unlikely that any such move will take place until damage has been very amply proved. Of course traffic is only one of the many sources of noise in built up areas. Neighbours who slam house and car doors, operate radios, television sets and record

[1] M. Morse, *The Unattached*, p. 215.

players at high volume, and indulge in strident rows or midnight parties can create more disturbance to others than steady traffic noise, partly because their outbursts often come so unexpectedly. It is easier to sleep or to concentrate throughout heavy traffic noise to which one is accustomed than through the break-up of a party or through the barking of a dog.

Here again it would be instructive to compare the school performances of children from quiet homes with those of children who live in noisy surroundings. We might find these latter more easily fatigued, more irritable and inattentive. Such an experiment would require full co-operation from parents since we should need to know when the children actually settled to sleep at night.

A phenomenon of city life akin to noise in its effects on people is the general overstimulation characteristic of our society. Many are being subjected to external stimuli throughout their waking hours, meeting other people's demands, or responding to a perpetual flow of messages from radio, television, newspapers and so on. Their attention is repeatedly snatched at from every side, so that in the course of a day they rarely relax entirely even for a few minutes. The outstanding case of this sort is the overworked mother of small children, or any conscientious mother who goes out to work. She knows only too well the feeling of being worried all the time by tasks competing for her attention. If, moreover, her way of spending such leisure as she does get is to play bingo, effectively, as long as she is awake, she never relaxes. Teachers with children of their own to go home to must be especially well acquainted with this situation of unremitting effort. In general women are more exposed to it than men and characteristically they are more inclined to respond to need until they drop in their tracks. (This feminine tendency may help to explain the greater prevalence of neurotic disturbance among women.) The housewife dreams of a life free from the demands of her children, yet so often when they have gone she finds herself no longer capable of yielding up her full attention to the books she has wanted to read, the music she has longed to listen to, the tutor of the class she has joined. She has become disturbance-addicted; lack of interruptions makes her uneasy. Almost everyone in our towns is in danger of becoming like this, through the incessant pressure from so many stimuli. It is a tiring way of life, with little satisfaction in it. We come to take it for granted that we should live in this manner and so become incapable of living in any other way. And then we wonder why we are devitalized, and what has become of the raptures and contentments we had expected. We have disqualified ourselves for experiencing them . . . or allowed circumstances to disqualify us.

Our urbanized society also tends to cut off its citizens from contact with nature, and so to weaken their impression of being part of it. Children from an inner ring London school, who were taken on holiday to the Isle of Wight in a school party, had never previously seen a daisy growing wild. To such as these, plants, animals or birds are exotic objects properly found in parks or zoos. For them the cycle of seasonal change is marked by hotter and colder, shorter nights or longer, but not by the maturing of the leaf, the flower and the fruit, not the mating songs of birds, nor the scrumping season for apples, nor the modest starting forth of next year's buds from the twig. All the unfolding drama of nature is missed, and with it the sense of participation in a mystery in which we too have our parts. To those who are aware of this drama, life is not long enough for marvelling at it, and their fellow creatures are worthy of respect as also belonging within it. But in the inner districts of our towns no amount of municipal grass sward can make up for the loss. What is the use of exhibiting nature as a system of great complexity if growing things are seen merely as specimens and there is no feeling of belonging to the system? The school's own garden is one answer to the problem, together with the class's own pet animals, window boxes on flats, an array of potted plants and caged birds such as are seen in the treeless tenement blocks of Venice and the Old Town in Lisbon. Reaching out for growing things of one's own to watch and enjoy is a healthy reaction to being shut up in an environment of concrete, brick and stone, and we must do all we can to encourage it, with visits to zoos and parks, school camps, walking holidays, instruction on the care of plants and captive animals. Nor should we neglect the study of the weather, since it helps to make sense of geography and sociology, and draws attention to the beauty of clouds and the slant of light, phenomena easily observed in the most built-up of towns. If people and nature are presented as a continuous whole, there is some hope of awakening a proper respect for everything that lives, a necessary undertaking now that formal religious belief is on the wane.

In support of my view that many city dwellers consciously feel starved of open space and the phenomena of wild nature, I should like to draw attention to the extraordinary success in cities like Birmingham of the film, *The Sound of Music*, which at the time of writing is in its third consecutive year at a single cinema. On January 11th 1967, a Midlands correspondent of *The Times* said of it:

'In the beginning it seemed to be just another film. One provincial critic is rumoured to have dismissed the thing as "a dim little flick". Nobody knew that the bounds of reason were about to be demolished by a social phenomenon disguised as light entertainment . . . bookings are coming in for next December. Anyone who wants to take a coach party on a Saturday night will have to wait until August. About 1,300,000 people have seen the film in Birmingham, with its population of 1,090,000 and hundreds were still being turned away from matinées in the Christmas holidays. Cardiff has a population of 256,000 and 954,775 people had seen the film there by the end of November. About 971,000 had seen it in Newcastle-on-Tyne . . . Last week *Variety*, the entertainment industry weekly, reported that *The Sound of Music* had surpassed *Gone with the Wind* as the biggest hit in film history. The question is, why? A number of women in the entrance hall of the cinema were asked why they were seeing this film again. One said: "You do get a sort of feeling of being carried away to Austria. When you leave the cinema you feel as if you had been in a different world." A pensioner living alone said she had seen it one hundred and twenty-one times, adding: "I love musicals, but there has been nothing to approach this one. It is gorgeous, it takes me right out of this world. It is the greatest joy and pleasure for me. I always say I am going to Austria for the afternoon when I come to see it." Its world is a place of blue skies and open mountainsides where children are good and happy and God is in his heaven. In this cold and concrete city, many of the people who come to see it are from lonely flats on new estates, from council houses with a view of chimneys and cooling towers, from Old Peoples' Homes. How far, perhaps, is the awful eagerness to see this pleasant film a sign that simple and basic things are lacking in many peoples' lives today?'

Geographical mobility from many causes has for some time been on the increase. People move about in search of work or promotion, they are moved by housing authorities to better dwellings often quite remote from where they lived before, sometimes in a New Town, or they become tired of the inconveniences of town life and move themselves into 'commuter country'. All of these migrations, we are told, tend to cause rootlessness. For in their new homes people often fail to make contact with their neighbours, take no part in communal life, achieve no sense of belonging to the locality. The evidence of Young and Willmott's *Family and Kinship in the East End of London* indicates that large numbers once they have left the warm inner ring communities where they were surrounded by relatives and childhood acquaintances, do not quickly join in the corporate life of the new housing estate in which they have been allotted a dwelling. To them their new neighbours are strangers, whom they feel they have to impress so as not to be looked down on by them. They are afraid that friendly overtures will be met with either rebuffs or exploitation. So instead begins the leapfrog pattern of the Smiths putting up the more expensive curtains, Jones laying out his garden more elaborately, Smith retaliating by triumphantly bringing home a new car, and so on without end. In this competitive game the children's examination results too play their part.

Insidiously this becomes one of the main interests in their lives. It is an interest which divides people into competing family units and impedes the formation of a corporate life. 'Dropping in' on relations and visits to the pub are now replaced by home decoration, gardening and television, all of them occupations pursued within the limits of the home. Outings in the family car, a sort of mobile parlour, are nothing but an extension of this tendency on the part of the nuclear family to draw back into itself.

The callous indifference of onlookers to distressing incidents may be an outcome of all this. In Bristol in September 1967 bus crews refused to work later than 9 p.m. because passengers would give them no help in dealing with young roughs who boarded the buses late at night. In the *Birmingham Mail* of September 19th, 1967 appears a letter signed 'Girl of Seventeen, Handsworth', in which she says 'Returning home to Handsworth about 7 p.m., I was suddenly grabbed by a man as I crossed Soho Road [the main road]. Despite my struggles I could not free myself. I was pretty frightened, as you can imagine, but not one person in this crowded road came to my assistance. As it happened I was lucky. My father was near and he chased the man away . . . To make matters worse as I walked away, some of the onlookers were actually laughing.' Sightseers with cars have blocked the roads around scenes of railway and aviation accidents and crowds went to Aberfan not to help in any way but simply to gape. The crowds of spectators who treat untoward happenings as free entertainment seem to have got much larger and more uncontrollable, often holding up the access of ambulances and fire brigades, and the unhelpful and unkind attitude of onlookers in general seems to be something new. It has all become more noticeable since increased geographical mobility has produced the phenomena of rootlessness and lack of corporate life. People are becoming conditioned to looking on instead of pulling their weight. Each nuclear family is a tight little knot, unconcerned with what goes on in the other little knots, satisfied with imitating other people instead of getting to know them.[1]

If this tendency should continue, the outlook for social life is bleak indeed. We do need people to take a kindly interest in all those others whom they still encounter in the shops or on the beaches. Because we were afraid that our elderly relations might impair our home life, we have put them at arm's length; on weekdays we send our children to school for the day; we have moved so far away from the rest of the extended family that is life has withered away. All this should have left us with far more time for our neighbours and acquaintances. Should we then go on cutting ourselves off into tiny groups crouched in front of television sets or inside family cars? Helping and being stimulated by other people does not mean being exploited by them, as so many seem to fear. People, once they have learned the knack, can do more for one

[1] J. & E. Newson, in *Infant Care in an Urban Community* (1963), argue that the working-class wife today really expects to find her main source of satisfaction in her family, however small.

another than pep pills or sedatives, and social and ethical training in schools should prepare them for this.

By way of contrast it is worth while to cast a glance at the recent single class suburban developments in the U.S.A., where people live side by side with others of their own income group and to a considerable extent share their interests and habits.[1] On the surface at least there is not the mutual distrust that is so common among English neighbours; nearly everyone joins in the neighbourhood activities, the wives' morning coffee parties, the parent-teacher associations, the money-raising stunts for local amenities. There are sports clubs and dramatic societies. Children and young people move freely in and out of one another's houses, raiding the nearest refrigerator when they are hungry. There are communal picnics, 'shower parties' for engaged couples, and so on. We in England may feel that this way of life is somewhat extreme, leaving too little scope for individual difference. We would shrink from having to explain to gregarious neighbours our need for frequent quiet evenings with a book or the Hi-Fi. If indeed our tastes are for the sort of leisure occupation which calls for privacy, then our objection to overmuch communal activity is justifiable. But if we only want to shut ourselves up to watch television, perhaps we are making a big mistake; we might get more out of life if we did join in some group activities.

As things stand in most English suburbs, it is not too easy to get real companionship from the neighbours. Many have lost the habit of church-going with its affiliated group activities, which still persists in the U.S.A. Few of our community centres have been as successful as planners expected them to be. The towns lack any live counterpart for the rural Women's Institutes, which bring together women of all social classes. Membership of evening classes does a little, but not much, in giving rise to friendships. (I speak from observation of the behaviour of students in many cheerful classes that I have tutored since 1946. Class meetings were often followed by informal coffee parties. Yet despite the friendly atmosphere people did not appear to meet outside class evenings although I myself made many friends in this way.)

[1] W. Whyte, *Organization Man*, ch. 25 and 26.

The stream of social life in England seems to run rather shallow, so that many people do not readily make friends outside their own profession once adolescence is past. Yet getting to know other people intimately can be increasingly rewarding as we all grow older and develop into individuals with strong flavours of our own. It does seem perverse to limit our aquaintance with human nature to the immediate family circle, to TV personalities who are notoriously artificial, and the creations of novelists. Tiresome as it can be, village and small town life does at least give us a cross section of society to observe at close quarters and this is one of its real advantages. Yet what we need is not so much observation of others (however intelligent and appreciative), as a more direct participation in their lives. Friends heighten our pleasure in our successes and can share our griefs. If we have the courage to be candid all of us can learn by one another's experiences. The predicament we know to be shared is the less constricting for it, and collective exploration of ways and means does often yield solutions to problems. So, those who 'keep themselves to themselves' actually lose by their policy. It is noticeable that English people are at their most gregarious, most prone to form relationships with both sexes, during adolescence. Once they have got married, the exigencies of raising a family tend to isolate the English couple; this is especially so in the working classes.[1] Nor does our tradition sufficiently emphasize the expansion of interests and formation of new relationships which could take place when the children are older. In school, through sociometric groupings and group project work, we try to habituate children to co-operating with enjoyment. Perhaps we need to go further and suggest to them at every opportunity that genuine friendship, though it costs efforts and sacrifices, is worth every one of them, and that it is possible with those who are older or younger than ourselves, and at every stage of life. We should be doing something to militate against the rootlessness of our time by familiarizing them with the idea that wherever one happens to be, it is possible to reach out and make friends. And

---

[1] cf. Hannah Gavron, *The Captive Wife*. Two-thirds of the author's sample of working class mothers of young children did not make friends outside the family and 44 per cent of them said that they *never* went out in the evening: 71 per cent said they had no contact with their neighbours.

with present day communications it is no longer so difficult to keep in touch with those we already have when circumstances separate us from them. Telephones, motor-cars and spare beds or put-u-up settees are no longer limited to the middle classes.

I have been drawing attention to some generally recognized aspects of English urban life today. These increases in overcrowding, noise and general over-stimulation combine with the isolation of the towndweller from other non-human living things and with his being more frequently uprooted from familiar surroundings to constrain him towards that shallow and devitalized way of life which many teachers have regretfully noticed in their charges, and in the youngsters' parents as well. There is no longer the feeling of unrestricted freedom of movement for the individual on his own feet. Either he stays put in a smallish box, or he travels in a yet smaller box to and from further boxes for work or school, and to escape from his sensations of being shut in, he spends his leisure staring at the moving shadows of the household's entertainment box. He has departed a long way from the more natural life of thirty to forty years ago, when people walked freely about the towns they lived in, and streets and parks were altogether more intensively used as extensions for the home. Sound radio used to make more of a claim on the imaginations of its audience and less of a substitute for direct living than the hypnotic little screen which is taking over so many lives and sapping them of the initiative to do things and see things for themselves. People of all age-groups are thus having the scope of their lives quite drastically narrowed for them at the very time when one would have supposed that modern inventions and conveniences should be enlarging it. Teachers have commented to me that whereas when they were bored in school they filled in time by planning all the things they would *do* as soon as they got outside, their pupils today appear to have nothing of the sort in mind, and no place to go save home, which they make for at once, for the most part with television programmes in prospect. On one new housing estate, where the school tried to get a Third Session going, only twos and threes turned up for the various hobby groups. There is in many children a growing disinclination to lead active lives. They haven't the space, and the impulse itself is beginning to flag. Among city adolescents we often find a violent reaction against this situation, a sort of last fling which in 'Seagate' in Mary Morse's study of *The Unattached* takes the form of rushing around in bunches desperately searching for 'A Party' where real life, it is felt, must still be going on.[1] Much of the boredom and restless dissatisfaction of uncommitted teenagers may be seen as their form of protesting that 'There Must Be Something More'. Our present way of life in towns seems to be perpetuating a basically unsatisfied quality of experience to which every other factor I have mentioned contributes. One feels that our schools could be equipping young people far better than they have done so far to stand up to these pressures of urbanized life.

[1] Mary Morse, *The Unattached*, pp. 38–40.

III · Basic Intellectual Training

In a technically complex and rapidly changing society we need technically-minded, alert and adaptable people. The faster the rate of change the more we must work to equip young people to adapt to it both in their jobs and as consumers; we need their adaptability and trained intelligence on the job and they themselves need both as consumers. From the day that they enter their first school we should be encouraging them to recognize problems and solve them. In education we owe it to the young to show them how to use their mother wit so that they may lead more satisfying lives; our emphasis should be less academic, more practical than it has commonly been so far. We want to train them to live as well as to pass examinations.

It is already commonly assumed today that during their last two years at school youngsters who are not working for public examinations should receive some training relevant to the sort of job they hope to do. Thus there are preliminary courses for intending clerical workers, shop assistants, nursing auxiliaries, even bricklayers (in at least one Birmingham school). Now all of this is useful as giving young people some assurance that the last year or two of school life is no mere waste of time; in school they can already be learning something of a general approach to the work they will do, its advantages and difficulties for them personally. Typing, shorthand, book-keeping, first aid, hygiene, sales procedure etc. can to a considerable extent be taught in the classroom. Nevertheless it should be made clear that what is undertaken in schools is only in the nature of a preliminary canter for the young worker. For in schools we cannot reproduce the working conditions of the actual shop, office, hospital or workshop, nor convey the impression of what it is like suddenly to have hours of work extended to a steady seven or eight per day. We are merely providing samples rather than the thing itself, the job under normal conditions. Our samples are better than no preparation at all. But shouldn't we also be trying to discover and explain the differences between the ethic of school and that of the workplace, between classroom procedure and those of factory, office and shop? Perhaps more of the teachers should have experience of these working environments, enabling them to clarify such differences for their pupils. For instance, an anthropological discussion of the barbaric initiation procedures for apprentices in some trades might enable boys to take them more dispassionately, be less committed by them to an obsolescent tradition of male brutality.

Certainly in school we can accustom young people to working with their hands dexterously and precisely. We can give them the confidence that comes of successful use of tools, of making something oneself and doing it well. That confidence is worth having, for it adds immeasurably to one's self respect, one's satisfaction with life and one's sense of security. Without any skills it is only too easy to feel lost in the world of today, useless, ignorant, the dupe of others who will charge one a heavy price for the exercise of *their* skills in one's service. But it should be generally understood that school handicrafts are more useful as training for the domestic handyman than as preparation for a job. It is impossible to fit up a classroom as a modern workshop and given the present rate of technical change, the techniques learned in school may soon be obsolete. Nevertheless in school it should be possible to acquire the *approach* of a craftsman and so be ready to pass on from exercising one skill to exercising others. In school, too, people can get a working knowledge of the principles of dynamics and electrical phenomena, enabling them to grasp more easily the functioning of machinery or gadgets they will later come to use. Modern methods of science teaching which progress from the particular problem to the underlying principles should help them to tackle difficulties intelligently as they arise. Given the craft experience in school along with scientific teaching directed to the explanation of mechanical and electrical devices, young people when they leave school could be equipped to live more competently than their predecessors in an era of technical development, to be more readily trainable for a variety of jobs, and not to be at the mercy of unscrupulous or careless advertisers and salesmen.

Just as before the war people were able to live in much the same way for decades together, in those days it was still possible for numerous jobs to be 'picked up' by a boy following some skilled man around as he worked, holding his tools and looking on. To a greater extent today, this form of 'training' is unsatisfactory in that the beginner does not necessarily get told *why* the job should be done in that way: the skilled man may be incapable of explaining clearly. It is increasingly important for everyone to be imbued early in life with the desire to understand how things happen and why they happen as they do. For this reason it is more useful to start childrens' minds working inferentially than to cram them with facts.

Until quite recently, many schools have neglected training in logic, by which I do not mean formal logic whether Aristotelian or Russellian, nor the logic of Euclid, but inductive logic at an elementary level, enabling people to make reasonable inferences from the facts at their disposal to all kinds of other factual situations which may be relevant to their interests. Of course there are some children who are not capable of much in this line. But all save the tragically defective must be capable of surpassing the performance of animals. An animal learns to interpret clues in his environment as to what he may expect. Properly motivated, children can do the same. Part of the business of the teacher is to induce children to form the habit of looking for the significance of what they observe. That this kind of training is neglected in schools is clear from the frequency with which people fail to infer the obvious. There can be few of us who have not sometimes failed in this way, to our disadvantage. Our only comfort may be that we see others equally obtuse. In sum, failure to infer the obvious accounts for a great amount of human misery.

There is plenty of scope for developing the habit of inferring from available facts in the course of school work on practical projects, and in Nuffield science. But what is wanted is the beginnings at a very elementary level as soon as children have settled down at school. No provision was made for anything of the sort in any of the schools I attended, including that which was reputed to be the best in its city. Yet it would be simple for any teacher whose attention had been directed to the need for it to train children in the habit of working things out for themselves. It can begin as a game, taken up many times in a day, of 'How do you suppose this has happened?', 'What will probably happen if we . . .?', 'Where can this have come from? How?' and so on. For instance, 'How did this paint mark get onto the *back* of Julie's dress?' 'What will happen to things on the bench under the windows if we leave them open while it is raining?'. . . or, if the windows are so designed as to prevent this from occurring: 'Why is it safe to leave things here with the windows open even when it rains?' and 'How did the water get into the bottom of the bucket?' and 'What do you think will happen to me if I go out into the snow in these shoes?' Opportunities for inference-games arise all day long in any classroom whose inhabitants are not completely petrified. The greater the degree of child-activity, the more the occasions for making inferences.[1] Some children will always be ready with an answer; others will need repeated stimulation. The important thing is that the habit of noticing things and making inferences from them should be thoroughly instilled. Without it the acquisition of facts is almost useless. I would rank it with literacy and numeracy as a basic aptitude which junior schools should have inculcated in every child before he goes on to secondary level. Without it children's 'guided exploration' of their environment in classroom and library will not lead very far. But at every level the teacher must go back over the work in progress and ask the pupil, 'How did you (or your friends) come by this idea?' There could hardly be too much insistence on inferential process. Hitherto the learning of school subjects below the advanced level (apart from mathematics) has made little call on it and this is why in my own schooldays it was neglected. One has to be *told* the facts of grammar, history or botany, one cannot infer them from anything. But today with the general introduction of the project approach there can be altogether more emphasis on *putting to work* the facts which can be looked up in the library or found in the newspapers. Given the accessible facts, pupils in their early teens should be led to infer for themselves what will be the population situation in this country by the time they are in their forties, and what will be the traffic

---

[1] Excellent opportunities for this sort of activity would be afforded by the I.D.E. group-project type of work sponsored by the Curriculum Laboratory of Goldsmiths' College, London. see pp. 140 *et seq* below.

situation, and how these matters are likely to affect the lives of everyone. The boy of average ability, by the time he leaves school, should be capable of finding the answer to such problems as this: In looking over a house that is for sale, what do you infer from the facts that the dining-room (which is separate from the sitting-room) faces north, looks as though it had been little used . . . paint-work in good condition but not very fresh . . . and has some floor-boards in the bay which are differently stained from the rest? Or again: What do you infer from the presence of barbed wire on the fencing between this garden and the next? Of barbed wire on all the fencing around this garden? Most girls thoroughly enjoy pursuing in this way the probabilities of some person's behaviour as inferred from his past conduct.

Literacy and numeracy work together with the habit of inference to equip a youngster to cope with the environment of a modern technological society. Top priority really should be given to establishing literacy and numeracy as early as possible in every child's school life, since without them he cannot make much progress. It is hardly fair to secondary school teachers to thrust on them year after year a deadweight of young incompetents, as John Partridge says of those in their third and fourth years: 'Nobody really knows how to teach boys who are at best only semi-literate; and few teachers wish to devote themselves to so exhausting and frustrating a task, so that any activity which keeps D and C boys quiet is looked upon as admirable. Inevitably some of these boys become the oddjobmen of the School. This means that the contrast between the standards of literacy of the best and worst classes becomes even more marked as boys progress through the School; the better pupils are pushed steadily along, the worst are not pushed at all, and so the gap grows'.[1] Discipline in these lower streams as he points out is bad. The D class tends 'to choose as its unofficial spokesmen the more antisocial elements'.[2] and to be 'hostile to learning in general and teachers in particular'.[3] 'Since low stream classes are difficult to control most of the time, it is not surprising that D boys in particular are left out of many school

[1] J. Partridge, *Middle School*, p. 84.
[2] Ibid, p. 76.
[3] Ibid, p. 72.

activities. When there was not room for all the classes at the swim-
ming baths, it was the remove who were not allowed to go; when
the film of Shakespeare's *Julius Caesar* was shown in the school
hall it was 4D who did not see it. D classes tend to go on fewer
school excursions or educational visits than other classes.' From
the evidence of Partridge on this one secondary modern school
(which is by no means unrepresentative, to judge by what I have
seen and heard) teachers in infant and junior schools should take
warning as to what lies ahead for such of their own leavers as have
failed for whatever reason to learn to read, write and do arithmetic
with reasonable competence. These children fail to pass the eleven-
plus examination or to reach the upper streams in secondary
modern or comprehensive schools. Trapped in the lower streams
they fall ever farther behind their luckier contemporaries. Needing
more practice than others rather than less, they are written off as
hopeless, and 'less' is henceforward their fate all along the way. It
seems reckless to send children on to secondary school unfit to
profit by what it offers.[1] Many secondary schools find themselves
unable to provide all the remedial classes that would be required to
bring their intake up to the level at which secondary work begins.
Although they may try to undertake this task, it does not properly
belong to them. And children who cannot read are much more
difficult to keep occupied once they have passed the biddable age.
Not being literate and numerate at an age at which most of their
contemporaries already are, makes them quietly desperate, and
too often the only way out is not to care.

The primary teacher has the easier job in that he does not have
to cope with these problems of pupil resistance on the same scale.
For his charges are as yet relatively docile and keen to please him,
and the atmosphere of the primary school is normally altogether
more relaxed. He has therefore better opportunities for insisting
that his charges should master the basic skills. Of almost every
child who is not doing this it is legitimate to ask, 'Will this one end
in an approved school or a Borstal?' Before he is over the age of
eight each slow learner should have been noticed and given massive

---

[1] Anthony Hurst in 'Help for the Illiterates' (*New Society*, vol. VIII, 1st September 1966) estimated that 37 per cent of children in south west London were
leaving school still illiterate.

extra help. Where learning through play and through discovery have not paid dividends, steady application may have to replace them for a while. Children who read badly cannot spare so much time as others for work that does not involve reading. There will be plenty of time for other activities later on, but reading, writing and arithmetic cannot wait, since they are the pre-requisites of almost all further work in school, and the only means to avoid the distressing situation described by Partridge. Sad though it is to have to say so, there are children who cannot afford to do a wide range of things while in primary school. These are the ones who need training to do a few things thoroughly, and those things certainly include the three Rs. I would not be taken to mean that these must be taught in the old manner as boring drills, exercises undertaken in a void serving no object outside literacy and numeracy; they must always be part of wider activities of exploring the world around us. But the emphasis clearly needs to lie, for slow learners, on getting the reading and writing actually done, the calculations performed, and not occasionally in the course of a project but steadily, day in day out. The project has to grow, to show a deal of work achieved, before it can be laid aside for something else. Time must not be allowed to slip away in looking at books that are never actually read or in talking over what might be done without at least attempting to do it. One cannot but suspect that it is here that the weakness lies, in inadequate supervision of the many individual undertakings of primary school children working on their own. One is also tempted to wonder whether play activities are allowed to continue too long into the school life of the slow learner, and whether the teacher is always able to detect the moment at which the child is genuinely ready to move on to systematic work. (There have been cases of children whose teachers maintained that they were not yet ready to read although they had actually been reading at home for some time.) If children are not pressed to work, many of them will be quite happy not to begin. The classroom atmosphere will be relaxed and pleasant, the children will enjoy it and so will the teacher, but some will not be exerting themselves nearly enough, and later on it will be harder for them and for their teachers. As the Plowden Committee says, 'Many infant schools are outstanding for the quality of the relationships between teachers and children. They excel in the opportunities they provide for play and the talk that accompanies it, the stress they put on individual learning, and the skill with which teachers select from the various methods of teaching reading those that suit themselves and the individual children.' Yet 'there is overwhelming evidence that many children have not achieved a mastery of reading by the time they leave the infant school'. A reading survey conducted by the N.F.E.R. in Kent showed that . . . 45 per cent of the children in the first year junior classes still needed the kind of teaching which is to be found in infant schools. Yet most of their teachers had received no training in infant methods and a substantial minority had no knowledge of how to teach the beginnings of reading. The survey also demonstrated that the prospects of success in reading for children who are poor readers when they transfer to the junior school are very gloomy indeed.[1] It looks as though the specialists in teaching the beginnings of reading have not been doing their stuff. The Plowden Committee conclude that children should have three years in infant school so as to ensure that they can read on transfer to the junior school. This seems a fair recognition of the primary importance of literacy.

Another part of intellectual training which should be undertaken early in schooling is habituating children to carry on with any project once they have begun it. A multitude of beginnings begets the butterfly mind, always on the lookout for a distraction, only too ready to leave the matter in hand for something else. Almost anybody can *begin* something: what is so much harder is persisting with it to a satisfactory conclusion. And this is very much a matter of habit. Every time we finish a task we make it that much easier for ourselves to persist with the next one and every time we leave something unfinished we increase our own inclination to leave other jobs half done. Perseverance is something which surely can be encouraged in school, and to that end some junior schools have begun to experiment with highly flexible time-tabling, enabling each child to choose his work and go on with it until he has exhausted his interest in it. This is an advance on rigid time-tables

[1] Plowden Report. Vol I. Paragraphs 361–3. Also Joyce Morris: *Standards and Progress in Reading*, N.F.E.R. 1966.

which break the school day into short periods so that interest that has been aroused is squandered as everything is cleared away for the next lesson. We do not know what the individual child's span of attention is likely to be until we have got him moving on something which really absorbs him. Surely it is a vital function of education to find out what activities *can* thus engage his attention, and to give him opportunities for pursuing them? Those children who will not settle to anything, but disturb others at their work, may need to be removed from the room where their class mates are seriously occupied.

Objections to the policy of allowing children to fix their own hours of work lie chiefly in the responsibility laid on the teacher to keep careful records of what each pupil is doing and persuade him to balance his activities so that nothing essential gets omitted. The child weak in numeracy cannot be left to please himself as to whether he gets enough mathematical activity to remedy his weakness; the need to arouse his interest in this field is urgent and may demand considerable ingenuity. Indeed, while still in their earlier years of school, children have to face the unpleasant necessity of working at tasks they find neither easy nor attractive; the child who was spared this necessity in school would be very ill-prepared for life as most people live it, and would inevitably find it hard to get a grip on everyday situations. Skilfully handled, project work can involve pupils in tackling their own difficulties courageously.

Allowing them to make their own time-table is an expedient for strengthening power of attention by not letting it be frittered away on a rapid succession of multifarious activities. Arousing attention in the first place is one problem: fixing it when aroused is another. The rousing of attention presents little difficulty to an experienced teacher with a normal child: the fixing of attention is one of the problems of our time in all age groups. You can catch a child's interest with anything new and stimulating, but how do you fix it to the degree that is requisite if he is to go on to work eagerly on his own and in spite of difficulties? Many children will need long conversations with the teacher in the course of which interests they already have can be identified and linked with the work on hand. Each when he flags will need restimulating with relevant suggestions. It is easy to talk about the teacher's role in this situation, but hard for the teacher himself to fulfil it. Yet unless he is fairly successful in this sort of undertaking, some of his pupils may miss their chance of discovering what they can do and of enjoying the work *as* a job undertaken and completed. With every technique we can think of we should be coaxing children into focussing their attention and keeping it undistracted, so that they form the habit of persisting with each project until it can be thought of as complete. There is no other way of combating the threat to full and rewarding living that the butterfly mind presents, a threat that is aggravated by the constant over-stimulation of the urban environment.

Something is sadly wrong with people who are so dependent on an unending succession of external stimuli that the failure of the television set opens a yawning gap in their lives and they cannot settle to work without 'musak' or a transistor radio to jolly them along. A research worker in physiology told me that she had been horrified to discover that she had reached the point at which she paid only a minimal attention to her surroundings when not actually at work, her mind being apparently fixed on a popular song which she went over again and again. When she questioned the people she worked with, she found that many of them had similar experiences. They did not like to carry transistor sets with them but the internal hum seemed to fulfil the same function, of keeping the mind occupied with trivialities, creating the illusion that something significant was happening. They preferred this to the exertion of actually thinking for themselves, of taking the initiative, of applying themselves to something. Their habitual condition was neither one of absorbing activity nor one of repose. This would not be surprising in the disturbance-addicted housewife mentioned in an earlier chapter, but is hardly appropriate to highly trained research workers who ought to be capable of alternating the kind of attention which excludes distractions with genuine relaxation. They seemed to feel the need to be always at half-cock, neither at rest nor alert. This is somehow connected with the amount of distraction which people today seem to find normal, preventing them from either working to full capacity, the mind focussed on its object and gathering in relevant suggestions at all levels, or reposing calmly without any felt need for a distraction. Some adults who become aware of this condition seek to remedy it by Yoga training. It would be preferable to foster the power of concentration in schoolchildren so that they would become less liable to the malady of half-attention.

In our care for the quality of children's day-to-day experience, we ought to try harder to cut down classroom noise, which tires people whether they knew it or not. If the school room is the only place where they can experience a therapy of silence, it is all the more important that that room should be silent or nearly so. The 'silence zones' of open plan schools will indeed require good insulation from sound. It is hard to concentrate on a task from which the mind already has some tendency to flinch when one can hear somebody practising the recorder. A teacher who does not himself mind the hubbub in his classroom may still be impairing the efforts of such of his pupils as do. I am not suggesting that we go back to that deathly stillness in which a pin could be heard falling, which used to be considered the hallmark of effective classroom discipline. Yet the volume of conversation and other activities ought not to exceed that level which is tolerable to the more easily distracted and those sensitive to noise. And when the teacher is addressing the entire class, what excuse could there be for *any* other voice being heard? The home that is too noisy for effective study needs to be supplemented by silent and supervised preparation rooms in school, open during the evenings. What is important is that no child should be without the opportunity to work quietly on his own.

Finally it seems worthwhile to comment on the current tendency to denounce the memorizing of material as useless. It is of course vital that memorized information should be seen to be relevant to the needs and interests of the pupils. It is for instance manifestly absurd that they should be set to learn about tea growing in China and the climatic conditions conducive to success in it, rather than barley or rose-growing in Britain, and the climatic conditions of various districts in the British Isles. Given that memorizing is of data for which the pupil might some day have a use, there is much to be said on its behalf. While it is true that ability to speak or write down correctly upon demand large amounts of memorized information indicates little about the quality of the pupil's mind, his

ability to synthesize or to ask pertinent questions, nevertheless it
does reveal whether or not he has paid attention to what he has
read or been told, whether he has done some work or none within
the area designated, and that he is at least capable of accuracy.
Moreover, without being in possession of detailed information
with which he is so familiar that he does not need to look for it in
books, but can marshal it effectively at will for purposes of com-
parison-making, nobody could do any genuine synthetic theorising.
A foundation of factual knowledge must be present before interesting constructions can be begun. The medical practitioner seeking
to diagnose a patient's condition must know so well the structure
and functioning of the human body and the many signs of deviation from what is taken as normal that he can draw on his knowledge without hesitation. The botanist must know all the minute
variations in structure by which plants are classified before he can
confidently recognize a specimen as a new variety. The linguist
must have digested many syntactical and inflectional devices in a
particular language before he can be sure of the exact meaning to
be attributed to this or that sentence. Even in the everyday study
of human character a wealth of patiently observed detail recalled,
albeit unconsciously, underlies every valid judgement that we
make. Without memory-recall at some level of awareness, there
could be no knowledge of any kind, even in the fields of logic and
mathematics. And we cannot rely on acquiring the relevant data
by osmosis from our environment, too little comes that way for
most purposes. There has to be some resort to rote-learning. In
arithmetic, memorized tables of multiplication and addition
patterns save endless time and labour. We cannot speak with scorn
of mere computation as though everyone had an adding machine at
his elbow perpetually: we all need to check by calculations of our
own the sums done by the milkman and the shop-assistant,
since only too often these too are weak on their tables. We have to
be able to work out how much wallpaper and how much paint to
buy for the room we propose to decorate, how much wood or how
many ounces of wool we need for such and such a job. Which shop
offers us the most profitable terms? At what point in its working life
would it pay us to replace a given implement? Such questions will
not be answered without computations that we perform for ourselves.

Although children should not be crammed with facts and formulae to the exclusion of individual interests and judgement, neither should they be unaccustomed to the tasks of memorizing and computing, nor so devoid of memorized data that everything has to be looked up every time. There is no antithesis between being well instructed and being creative. Information relevant to the task in hand and well brooded over, plus the abilities to infer and to calculate correctly are pre-requisites of any real progress. What is the evidence that imitation and the following of an experienced guide in the early stages of a study inhibits originality? Raphael learned to paint in his own style by first painting in the idiom of Perugino. In the days of individualized handwritings everyone began by copying the copperplate model and those who were capable of it later modified it into a wide variety of 'hands' expressing their own characters. At the same time, pupils ought to be assessed and examined on their logical and critical powers and their flair for theory-building, as well as on their computational accuracy and powers of memory-recall. They should be required to *put to work* those facts that they have retained.

I am arguing that everyone who is not 'subnormal' should leave school literate and numerate, trained in habits of practical inference, and able both to concentrate on work in hand and to carry it to a conclusion. This is the least that is required of members of a highly technical society.

IV · Widening the Range of Aesthetic Experience

Where there is not much room for movement, people will be obliged to have recourse to interests which do not require much space. Watching television as I have already pointed out is the easy way out. But it is an unsatisfactory one in that it turns its viewers into a passive audience, each feeding his own daydreams whereas he needs rather to find an occupation for his leisure which would exact from him an altogether bigger contribution. If Evening Institutes could provide lockers for work in progress and practice rooms to supplement class activities, then many more could pursue after school-leaving those crafts and hobbies begun in school. But there exist many interests which can stimulate the emotional and intellectual life without the use of much elbow-room . . . photography, sketching, music, serious reading, visits to theatre and cinema, chess, bridge, puzzle-solving, writing, embroidery. We ought to be encouraging young people to turn to these and extract from them the lifetime of satisfactions they can give. Enjoyment of art, of poetry, of all manner of literature and of visual impressions adds a dimension to the everyday experience with which it has been integrated.

In school we can begin to show children how to look at their surroundings simply for the pleasures of looking. Harmony of colour, shape and line are to be found or created everywhere about us, even in some townscapes of today, badly though we have been served by our planners. The clothes we wear, the decor of our homes, the lay-out of our gardens, all are material for aesthetic experience provided that we have been helped to see them that way.

Aesthetic education, like any other form of education, ought to last a lifetime. In school we lay its foundations and give the impetus to build on them incessantly. It should not be confined to the art room or the music class, for it crops up in the study of literature, in dressmaking, personal grooming, and every kind of craft work. Boys learning woodwork and metalwork must find out something about economy of design, about what constitutes a good shape for the object they are making, and how its functioning gives rise to beauty in the artefact. Most can appreciate the smooth working of the well made mechanism. Even the pleasure of a job properly done has its aesthetic aspect, for do we not speak of 'a lovely job'? All this can be initiated at school. Thus enjoyment of the sensory properties of things and of activities with or without reference to any purpose they may serve, can be deliberately cultivated in school to supplement the traditional sensualities of eating, drinking, tobacco, and lovemaking – the pleasures most widely resorted to and most frequently abused. A lively pleasure in the way things look or sound can never be abused, requires a minimum of space, and should be accessible to everyone.

It seems possible that through an unimaginative and conventional limitation of our materials, and an over-narrow interpretation of the nature of aesthetic experience, we have been failing to equip our young people to enjoy what is nowadays available to all, through the media of library books, paperbacks, museums, art exhibitions, broadcasts, or school excursions.

Some useful suggestions as to how aesthetic experiences of schoolchildren can be stimulated and made wider ranging and more detailed, are offered in the 'Creative Arts' example 4, of 'Work Now Being Done In Schools' in the Schools Council's Working Paper number 11, *Society and the Young School Leaver*. In the school whose work is described, Art and English are combined in a single department of 'Creative Arts' with a minimum of expository teaching. 'The aim is to place the pupil in a position where he has an immediate or vicarious experience, and then to challenge him to respond to it in the most vivid way possible.' For instance, children are asked to bicycle to a particular place and there observe and record specified points about the way it looks . . . the way the light shines through the leaves of the trees, the shapes of the trees themselves, their bark and leaves, how the colour of the sky and mood of the weather affect the appearances of the trees, and so on. In another exercise they are shown portraits by celebrated painters and asked to say what sort of person they feel the sitter must have been. In listening to 'programme music' they are asked to describe the pictures it suggests to them. In the art room they are told to study portraits by Augustus John and Stanley Spencer, and then to draw portraits of their own in similar detail, of a person whose appearance they have been describing with a view to indicating his character. They go on to study human bodily movements as signs of inward experience. The head of the department says, 'They are encouraged to see poetry almost as an expensive bottle of perfume, economical in words . . . Close your eyes, take the lid off and sniff. You have the evocation of the very soul of the contents . . . Good prose is the same; it can be impressionist like the art of Monet . . .' In this school children are really being shown how to look and listen, how to reflect and enjoy for themselves; the raw material is found sometimes in their own surroundings, sometimes in pictures or music that are presented to them, but whatever the material, they are stimulated to react to it individually and become aware of their own reactions. Thus the conviction is sown in them that aesthetic experience is within the compass of everyone, that it is an intimate aspect of living. We need far more work of this kind in our schools if our children are to learn how to live vividly in an environment that sets such physical limitations on them as our towns increasingly do today.

A fair enough question at this point would be 'Why shouldn't we rely on entertainment to make life palatable? What's wrong with entertainment? Most people think it's a very good thing. It's only cranks and crackpots who don't agree about this.' Here, with Plato[1] and J. S. Mill[2], I wish to argue that there really are 'higher' and 'lower' pleasures, even if the sole reason for making this distinction is the notable agreement between people of broad experience as to which pleasures are the most life-justifying. If people who are capable of enjoying both classical music and popular songs tell us that when faced with the decision which to listen to they most often choose the classical music, then we are justified in suspecting that the satisfactions given by classical music are in some way preferable to those given by a catchy tune. Perhaps they are more longlasting, bear repetition better without palling, are more

---

[1] Plato, *Republic*, Book IX, 580–8.
[2] J. S. Mill, *Utilitarianism*, ch. II.

complex . . . whatever the reason, they have more appeal for the ear and the mind that are trained and widely experienced. We may add that they have more subtleties to offer, take up the attention more completely and produce a profounder reaction, in anyone who is attuned to them. Further than this we can hardly go in arguing that some pleasures are higher than others. It is not however merely a matter of individual taste, but of the verdict of the collective taste of all those people who have really given themselves up to listening, looking, reading attentively and trying to understand. Such people do not tell us that the 'lower' pleasures are despicable, nor that all entertainment is trash. What they maintain is that there exist pleasures more deeply or exquisitely gratifying, whereas entertainment is an ephemeral interest only, and plays on our feelings superficially and crudely. It follows that if we want to taste more variously of the banquet that life sets before us, we must be prepared to train mind and sensibility to respond to the more complex stimuli of art and literature. We shall therefore not dally overlong at the level of mere entertainment, delightful as it can sometimes be. There must be room in our lives for both entertainment and art, and so we shall not let entertainment crowd art out of our experience. And this is the chief cause for complaint against entertainment, that it so often swallows up the leisure of people who are capable of enjoying something altogether more rewarding. It is as though these people perpetually refuse to grow up, staying at the level of pastimes fit for children, because these cost them less effort.

In people who thus fail to pass on from entertainment to genuine art, it may be that the imagination never quite succeeds in fulfilling its mature function. One of the best things in life is the vital interaction between the imagination and our sensory experiences, imagination adding a wealth of associations and comparisons to what we see and hear, and our seeings and hearings in turn touching off the imagination to flights of its own. Art and literature enrich this process by adding to the number of things we perceive which left to ourselves we should never have noticed, and by multiplying their associations and the reflections we are able to make on them. But entertainment, far from enriching the interaction, blocks it instead. How does it do this? By enclosing its audience in a sterile ring of over simplified images or stereotypes. They are so enticing, the images of entertainment, so bold, simple and gaily coloured (or cleanly black and white), that the slothful mind is only too glad to remain in the enchanted circle of these stereotypes, seeing and hearing entirely in terms of them, and accepting from sensory perception and emotional stimulation nothing that can substantially modify them. Thus the mind that is 'entertainment-bound' gradually loses the ability to learn through direct experience. But the man who is interested in genuine art and literature is always learning; he compares the subtleties found in books and paintings and statues with what he can observe for himself. Each illumines the other. The process is unending. So he never reaches the end of his interest in life. And this is what education ought to do for us, equip us so that our interest in life will never fail us.

People are often heard to say that they found some celebrated place disappointing, Venice for instance, or Florence: all they saw there was too many churches, too many people, and squalor. The reason for their disappointment is that they did not sufficiently prepare themselves before they went. They had not trained themselves to look properly, and so they did not recognize harmonies of form, colour and line. They were unable to reflect on what they saw with a well matured stock of ideas, concerning the history of the place, the functions of its numerous features, or the origins and parallels of their artistic styles. They were bound by the simplified entertainment-images of 'Venice' and 'Florence', with which those cities have little in common. The real place, like the paintings in its museums and churches, has been darkened by time and wear to a sombre richness that is far removed from the primary tints of the journalistic world. Even when all was new, it would still have differed from the glaring photographs of the travel posters, as noble cities and scenes must always differ from even the most evocative of photographs, by the sheer plenitude of its presence, a complexity from which the untrained mind recoils in fear of the effort needed for digesting so much that is unaccustomed.

There is also an inexplicable sense in which real art seems to point beyond itself at another world, whereas entertainment does not. This may be one of the things people have in mind when they speak of genuine art as 'profound' and entertainment as 'shallow'. Similarly experience that is said to be 'shallow' is experience that is among other things poor in associations, whereas profound experience is rich in associations, not to be confused with mere violence of feeling.

One of the tasks of education is to set the imagination to work creatively, feeding it with a variety of sensory and emotional experiences and encouraging it to transform them in its own way, which will be different for each individual child as he speaks or writes of what is most immediate and personal to him, instead of reproducing the hackneyed images he has picked up from journalism. The instance given in the Schools Council Working Paper quoted above indicate how the process can be begun. The important thing is to get each child perceiving life through his own point of view, his own accumulated experience, and not through the stereotypes of the entertainment world. The exercise has to be often repeated, in order to set the habit, so that its practitioners will develop into men and women who have little use for experience as mediated by entertainment. Why use the crude spectacles of *Red Sails in The Sunset* or *Coronation Street* when you could see through those of Shakespeare or Blake, and anyway you have eyes of your own?

Starved of its proper diet of external stimuli, such as the teacher in the first place may have to provide, the imagination may be dulled into quiescence as in the case of the West Indian children locked in their room sleeping while their mother was out at work.[1] Or grossly fed by entertainment it may burgeon in a riot of fantasy of a sort that makes no contribution to understanding of life-situations. I recall a great deal of this dead-end fantasy in my own childhood, peopled by the simulacra of persons seen only from a distance, or characters from children's storybooks, and I do not believe that I ever learned anything about either myself or the other characters from all the acting-out of my fantasies. I was well into my twenties before I had acquired the useful knack of elaborating imaginary conversations which really shed some light on my emotional involvements. So I am inclined to question the value of a good deal of childish fantasy; it seems to me a sort of safety valve, but

[1] see p. 85.

of little importance for actual learning. And if we supply it with too much material which bears a tenuous relation to real life, we may be encouraging children to linger in a shadow world when they might come out into the real one and learn how to savour that. What is so alarming about the dependence of many people of all age groups on the cruder offerings of the mass media is that instead of stimulating their imagination to further interaction with the actual environment, mere entertainment channels the imagination into an acting out of programme-based fantasies with oneself as the central figure, discovering nothing, noticing nothing, incapable of standing back and assessing what one is doing. Entertainment at its lowest level thus offers an insidious substitute for much of the real business of living, which is to discover, compare, assess, see, hear and touch with delight, distinguishing acutely for oneself by actual sensory experience.

In normal living we should all have our moments of triumph, but in our own persons not through identification with a hero-figure, and oftener through success in perfecting a technique or solving a problem than through outdoing a rival. We should all experience the self-transcending raptures of love, not in a shadow world but for real persons who might love us in return or at least be aware of our predicament and react to it. Frustration and loss are part of the raw material of life and can enrich even while they hurt; daydreams are *not* life, and if they are accepted in its place will end by crowding life out of the soul. We do not want to raise a generation potentially alienated from life and eager for the bizarre substitutes engendered by hashish and l.s.d. It is up to everyone to find love and friends and achievements of his own. The search may be long, one cannot predict that a soul-mate will turn up next Tuesday, but if the eyes are directed away from the external world the soul-mate may pass unrecognized this very day. We have to teach somehow the art of participating in life. The subtler and more suggestive television programme, the more adult novel, the genuine poem or musical composition, all can further this educative process as young people grapple with them and try to relate them to what they perceive of their own environments, which is progressively transformed through the struggles to extract a meaning. The interplay between art and the external world in one's mind is without end, the promise of interest continuing to the close of consciousness. Thus music, pictures, films, or books, far from being routes of escape become ways into life itself. A scene as presented in a work of art is amazingly complex and rich, and the setting-out point for many journeys of the mind; the same scene presented as entertainment is all too often reduced to a formula, thin and poor, part of a life so poverty stricken that to be palatable at all it must be irrigated with the firewater of violent primal emotions. In school we have to *move* children by literature, music and the visual arts until mere entertainment can no longer offer enough to give them a more than momentary pleasure.

It is clear that we must take great care in the choice of literature we offer in school. It should be selected for its potential value in illuminating the present and future experience of the children who study it. I well remember encountering in school set books that were far beyond my own emotional range not only at that time but for several years to come. This applies to the major tragedies of Shakespeare, even *Macbeth* which I met as an 'O' level text and saw at the time as a sort of western in gloomy surroundings. Similarly my husband 'did' both *Lear* and *Hamlet* at school, and gained very little from either, since *Hamlet* sets a thoroughly adult puzzle, and what can adolescent impatience be expected to make of *Lear*? My 'O' level texts went far to dampen my enthusiasm for literature and even to darken my outlook on life during my early teens: we had to study *Macbeth*, the poems of Matthew Arnold, and by way of light relief, the cynicism of *The School for Scandal*. In French, we read *Les Miserables*, another cheerless book. Who can have thought this a profitable or encouraging syllabus for fourteen- and fifteen-year-olds of the 1920s? The previous year we had plodded through *The Rape of the Lock* and to us it made little sense. Another bugbear had been a collection of longer narrative poems, none of which I have ever heard mentioned since. But the nadir of our literary experiences was certainly Livy, a dollop of which was set for 'O' level Latin. Who wants to know how many spears they had, or how many thousand paces they marched or what prisoners they took? The Romans seem to have had minds addicted to prosaic details. The next year we started on

Corneille and Racine, and the further we went with them, the less point I could see in it. Concluding that literature in any language was not for me, I left school before I had completed a term of the work for 'A' level. Yet since my schooldays I have had tremendous pleasure from reading both in English and French; I found that many of the 'classic writers' well deserved their reputations and that the texts set us in school had been unfortunate. Why introduce youngsters to such books, before their experience enables them to come to terms with them?

Some advance has indeed been made in this respect. The Joint Northern Board for 'O' level 1967 set as Shakespeare texts *Henry V* or *As You Like It* (Must there be a play by Shakespeare every year? Are there no other English playwrights?) The novels set were *Northanger Abbey* and *Kipps*, the poetry an anthology of twentieth century verse which includes work by De La Mare, T. S. Eliot and Robert Frost. The next year's menu includes *Romeo and Juliet* and *Animal Farm*. But each year there is also an alternative paper in modern literature, although some teachers suspect that the question-setters do not bear in mind the relative immaturity of 'O' level candidates. Why is the choice of set books so limited? On enquiry I discover that it is the schools themselves which limit it, for not only do teachers tell pupils which of the alternative set books they are to study, but they refrain from mentioning that under the regulations of the Joint Northern Board candidates may pay a little extra fee and propose their own set books. In a school with more than one 'O' level group reading English, there could be as many alternative texts as groups sitting the examination, named well beforehand to give a real choice, and fewer would find themselves committed to being examined on books which struck them as quite irrelevant to life as they know it. Surely in literature, as in art, music and crafts, we ought to avoid compelling young people to study something from which they can gain neither profit nor pleasure. There are doors which for some will never open, a fact that a successful system of options would allow for.

At bottom I am not happy about the conversion of works of art or literature into examinable courses of study, apart perhaps from the technical issues that they raise. 'Appreciation' should be undertaken for the sake of enjoyment, not to obtain a rating. Yet under the present rat race system, unless 'appreciation activities' are examinable many schools which set store by their academic successes will not teach them. Secondly, if there are to be any qualified teachers in the 'appreciation' subjects, these will have to be trained, and how else than by way of examinable courses at school and university level? Yet am I alone in finding it absurd that pupils should be compared and assessed with respect to their ability to enjoy something? How are we to avoid turning many of our students of literature into counterfeiters of enthusiasms that they do not feel? For an immature pupil is unlikely to be able to respond with spontaneous relish to writers as diverse as Shakespeare, Wells and T. S. Eliot. In training would-be teachers of literature it is surely more to the point to test them on ability to *arouse* interest and critical acumen in others, which cannot be properly done before they have had some teaching experience. What they could be examined on in the interim is factual and technical knowledge about literary works, plus powers of expression. Genuine feeling for literature or any other art is not invariably detectable in examination papers. Again, an examiner can hardly help assuming that good taste is that which agrees with his own. Even if he does not take this line, the candidates generally believe that he will. Wherever marks are awarded for having 'good taste', examinees have a strong incentive to find out the officially approved judgements and do their utmost to reproduce these. I. A. Richards in *Principles of Literary Criticism* found some Cambridge university students of English literature who had gone so far along this path that they were quite unable to produce a judgement of their own on specimen poems whose authors' names they did not know. Studying the official line is not the way to discover one's own reactions to a literary work. But the important thing is that students should react in their own way. A youth may be able to recapitulate with the utmost fluency the opinions of some fashionable critic on, let us say, George Eliot, but this is of far less value to him than his own attempt, however stumbling, to come to terms with her novels for himself. Yet in an examination paper it is very difficult to distinguish first-hand comment from restatement of other men's thoughts.

I have never seen it even hinted that, as individuals develop at very different rates there must be many who will find genuine pleasure in literature, painting or music only *after* they have left school. Even today (when physical maturity at least comes earlier in life) the late developer may still not have begun to enjoy any but the most unsophisticated items while at school and nevertheless still have before him the possibility of years of intense delight in the arts. We hear enough talk about intellectual late developers (although little is done to readmit them to our educational system once they have left it) but do we say often enough and seriously enough to school leavers that as they grow older they can expect to find their aesthetic tastes expanding and that they would be wise not to leave them undernourished? We have somehow to make a big dent in the working class view that interest in the arts is 'sissy' and is not for ordinary men and women. What is 'not for them' today may be 'for them' a few years hence, provided that they have developed no prejudice against it and are willing to look or listen or read receptively, building on the foundations we have laid in school. The arts reward those who genuinely seek them. Often in youth we seek in other directions, grasping for love, money or acclaim. The pleasures of contemplating things for their own sake are maturer pleasures, especially appropriate to that time of life when we no longer glory exclusively in our sexual prowess or in outdoing all comers. Some at least of our appetites are sated, or the sharpest edge is off them, and we have time to look more deeply into things. I am not for a moment suggesting that enjoyment of the arts cannot be intense in youth, but that unfortunately many people miss them altogether through not realizing that the capacity to delight in them may be late in developing. Young people characteristically cannot see far ahead. It has struck me that current emphasis on a youthful outlook may have the effect of preventing or discouraging many from maturing as they ought and leaving behind them without too much regret the satisfactions of youth so as to grow into those of middle age. Many modern parents set a poor example precisely because they themselves have failed to grow up and have stubbornly remained at the stage of an exclusive interest in entertainment. We want their children to go much further towards realizing *their* potential.

The English are an immature people many of whom have resisted education, living and dying at a level well below that of which they are capable.[1] School education is failing to ensure that they will keep on growing mentally and emotionally. Life presents to those who do not shrink from effort new wonders without end so that a man of forty can feel that he lives in a different world from that of his teens, not just a world that has moved on technically but one that has moreover been transformed for him personally by the changes in his own point of view and the growth of his appreciative powers. We should aim at conveying to young people the idea that to get stuck at any one stage is a waste of life, as each age group has its own satisfactions.

Every school needs its enthusiasts for art, pupils as well as staff, who are eager to share their enjoyment with others. Some who are unripe for these at sixteen may nevertheless bear in mind for half a lifetime how much the arts meant to others before coming at last to their own personal harvest of artistic pleasures. We have to indoctrinate, even at the level of delayed reaction, and to do it against the current of the mass culture which insists on easy satisfactions immediately available. We cannot afford to bow to fashion, if we really want to help our charges towards a fuller and deeper experience. But it is obviously expedient to introduce to young people the less sophisticated and more openly attractive works of art and literature before we try them with what is obscure or difficult and remote.

However much some people may despise it, even the snobs' way in to enjoyment of the arts has its uses. Given a powerful 'in-group' in the school community who lay claim to aesthetic interests – all the better if it includes athletes and school politicians – there are always those among the rank and file who will ape them by pretending to interests they do not actually share with them. Where the pretence involves concert going or visits to art exhibitions or the theatre, genuine appreciation may begin to emerge, if it is kept up long enough. Probably further education

[1] An excellent instance of this is to be found in the 'Seagate' group of young people who were 'basically dissatisfied, bored and resigned, with few prospects and no direction' but who were guided by a detached social worker into successful dramatic productions of which they had not realized they were capable. M. Morse, *The Unattached*, pp. 45–70.

of the 'sandwich-type' ought to include some cultural material alongside the vocational courses. A technical interest in the performance of high-fidelity equipment can lead on to an enjoyment of serious music, if only because it is intricately scored music which gives the apparatus its best opportunities for shining. Similarly some of the purchasers of elaborate photographic equipment for its prestige value will end by joining photographic societies to make the most of their new belongings and may eventually learn the fascination of good composition. The next step is to visit photographic exhibitions, after which the enthusiast for pictorial values finds his way to art galleries, and there have been those who have joined a painting group, relegating the camera to the office of taker of notes!

There must be tens of thousands of people for whom snobbery or the search for prestige-by-way-of-acquisition has thus become a gateway to aesthetic experience. Even the present craze for visiting stately homes puts into many heads new visions of visual harmonies in the domestic interior. It is plain that at the present day plenty of facilities exist for ordinary people who would like to extend their range of artistic experience. What we have to do in school is arouse the appetite for it.

V · Moral Training

Today it is a matter of common observation that there are parents who leave the moral training of their children to the schools. This is hard on the schools in view of the fact that the children may spend more of their waking hours at home than in school, so that it is the parents who actually have more time in which to influence them. Indeed, F. Musgrove points out in *The Family, Education and Society* that young people are more prone to adopt the values of their home environment than those of their school. It follows that no school is likely to have a strong moral influence on its pupils if it stands for an ethic that is quite opposed to that of their families. The neighbourhood school which aims at rehabilitating its catchment area must work tactfully, beginning from a moral position not too far removed from what is locally acceptable, and gradually upgrading it.

Nevertheless children in an overcrowded society have to learn to respect one another's needs. The more cramping the environment, the greater the demands it makes on our patience and forbearance with other people. We cannot make as much noise as we please, when flimsy partition walls between flats and terraced housing turn one listener's preferences into an ordeal unwillingly borne by dozens of others. The party late at night can disturb half a street. Our children should not play in the lifts and corridors of flat blocks; perhaps every flat block should have a sound-proofed rumpus room (with unbreakable windows through which the activities of the occupants can be seen!). In traffic, on sidewalks, in the stores, everywhere that we come into contact with others we need to think of the effects of what we do on *them*. All of this points to the need to instil into school children the principle of consideration for others. At present there seems to be a vogue among young people for the idea that it is possible to live in an urban society and please oneself without regard for consequences. The 'hippies' give an extreme expression to this tendency. Schools might head many young people off from certain misery for themselves and their friends if they could manage to give some currency to the view that nobody is an island. For instance, anyone who drives a motor vehicle is responsible for the lives and well-being of everyone he passes on his route. Some local authorities are keen that their school children should learn to drive. Are they equally keen on inculcating in them the appreciation of the responsibility they will then be undertaking?

The habit of taking into account the needs and the well-being of others can only be engrained by repeated discussion in class, utilizing instances as they arise many times a day in classroom practice, whatever the subject of the lesson. This turns every member of staff into a moral instructor and I can think of no other way of bringing it home to youngsters that we owe consideration to one another. Ethical teaching in schools cannot be limited to one lesson a week with the religious instruction specialist. The old classroom drill left no room for moral instruction aside from obedience to authority; the modern practice of working in groups does give a good teacher the opportunity to make the point that everyone should contribute to work that is afoot, neither being obstructive nor leaving everything to somebody else. This is basic training for citizenship and for co-operative family life (such as will increasingly be necessary when all married women go out to work). When people know how to operate as a team, life in the flat block or the crowded housing development can be conducted altogether more smoothly and pleasantly . . . with the proviso that the team are not combining to make life miserable for some outsider.

Perhaps the one true foundation for moral training is a proper respect for others as living beings on the same footing as oneself. One is tempted to have recourse to Charles Kingsley's Mrs Do-as-you-would-be-done-by and Mrs Be-done-by-as-you-did. Life in a crowded community cannot be carried on as a war of each against all, nor on the assumption that other people are just things to be pushed around and manipulated. To get these ideas firmly seated in children's minds can be expected to take the greater part of their school life, in small repeated doses. The feeling for one another as fellow men and women is properly part of religious

MORAL TRAINING   53

experience and a part that grows in importance as a consequence
of urban pressures. Yet the prevailing tendency today seems to be
towards nuclear families regarding themselves as in no way
responsible for anything outside their own home. The classic
instance of this attitude was the case a few years back of the
woman who was murdered in the street of an American town in
full view of a number of spectators in flats overlooking the scene,
who did not consider it their business. I suggest that we ought to
return to the doctrine that everyone is his brother's keeper.
Otherwise we are in serious danger of becoming like the chickens
who live isolated each in his tiny coop with wings and beaks
damaged through overcrowding, all squawking in wretchedness:
an unlovely prospect.

The way out seems to be to slant religious instruction towards
making young people aware of the unique value of every human
being. The old way of stating the position was by saying that we
are all God's creatures and as such have a right to one another's
respect. In a wholly secular-minded society the danger is that
people will come to be seen merely as means to one's own ends
instead of Ends in the Kingdom of Ends. Another difficulty
inherent in the technological secular society of today is that the
emphasis on innovations destroys respect for any traditional moral
code. There is a presumption that if anything is old, it must be out
of date. Young people in their eagerness to be 'with it' have little
use for the intuitionist view of ethics (as expounded for instance
by Butler and Kant) which is that any honest person by the use of
his own moral intuition or conscience will be able to perceive the
Moral Standards for himself. In practice this view of ethics has
normally been associated with acceptance of a religiously
authorized moral code such as the Ten Commandments, and it is
this code that is to be perceived. That is, moral perception is
equated with acceptance of a given set of rules. Today when many
teachers are not practising Christians and find the giving of
religious instruction repugnant, moral education may have to be
based on some other principle. It is here that the utilitarian
outlook comes into its own. Young people with whom the argument: 'X should not be done because it is *wrong*' (by Christian
standards) cuts no ice, may still be open to conviction by the

utilitarian argument: 'X should not be done *because it will do more harm than good*'. If you say to them 'It is wrong to smoke pot', they may feel that your words mean nothing, that you are merely making a ritual exclamation. At the most, they will have a vague impression of some obligation that seems to be binding on you but not on them. But if instead you can point to undoubted long term effects of pot-smoking and show that these amount to a rejection of life (productivity of harm), then you are more likely to convince uncertain youngsters. They will begin by exploring the situation through argument. For instance they may maintain that one has the right to opt for lotus eating. But as they go on looking the possibilities in the face, most of them will end by agreeing that pot-smoking is a dangerous habit, a risk not worth taking. The word 'wrong' which to them suggested no more than a vague uneasiness (if so much as that), has been replaced by the word 'dangerous', with vivid ideas of the psychological addiction created by the marihuana habit, and the accompanying lethargy and self-neglect. Of course a great deal depends on the conviction and practical knowledge of the teacher. Unless he knows what he is talking about, he will himself be unable to press the utilitarian line of argument. This points clearly to the need for a high level of intelligence and probity among those teachers most responsible for moral training . . . and these will include everyone teaching the 'humanities' or non-scientific subjects. The failure of education in England today to induce young people to think and judge in moral terms is very disturbing . . . this is one of those respects in which the English may be regarded as uneducated. In our colleges of education we should be making a serious effort to show trainee teachers how to induce a moral habit of thought in their pupils. Today this means that we must accustom intending teachers to utilitarian ways of thinking such as are likely to have most effect on the children of today (and of tomorrow if present trends continue).

Briefly, the utilitarian approach is the habit of trying to assess whatever we do or see others do in terms of its probable effects on people – not merely on oneself but on anyone who stands to be affected. Thus if I park my car where it can obstruct traffic flow in a narrow or very busy street, it is obvious to anyone who thinks about my action that it shows disregard for the convenience and even the safety of other people. When I return to the scene to find police and ambulance men at work, 'I did not think' is not a satisfactory answer to the question: 'Why did you have to leave it just there?' nor is 'I did not care'. I *ought* to have thought and to have cared, even if that would have involved me in walking another couple of blocks. The moral aspect of the situation lies in paying heed to the probable effects of one's conduct on *other people*. A good man tries to foresee the consequences of what he does and to maximize the excess of happiness over unhappiness, and of well-being over misery. When we are inexperienced, virtue on these lines certainly involves great effort in thinking round each situation and trying to foresee the outcome of alternative courses of action. This is where the old accepted moral rules still have their usefulness in showing which kinds of conduct have been found most productive of happiness. The younger we are, the more helpful these rules as indications of the best line to follow. It is only after years of observing events that we are really in a position to back our *own* moral judgement as against established rules. This point needs to be made to young people by every means at our disposal. Growing up should be seen to mean accumulating more experience of the courses that events take, and so of improving one's judgement as to the most beneficial lines of action. It takes a very experienced person to break moral rules with justification. So being young and 'with it', heedless of rules or of the wisdom of those who *have* succeeded in growing up (and of course some people never do), may come to be recognized as being impelled to act blindly. This puts on teachers a heavy onus to show themselves at least a little more mature than their pupils. They have to be people of more exercised judgement than those they are teaching, people who are convinced of the importance of learning how to live. There is no proper place in the teaching profession for moral or practical duffers. Youngsters do ultimately recognize sound and convinced judgement and are inclined to defer to its authority, but for waverers they have no respect. In a sense the function of the teacher is to lead by his own example, and not merely to exhort.

The utilitarian way of thought is a vital extension of what I have already described under the heading of practical inference, involving as it does both observation of situations and inference from them of further possibilities. I believe that children should be introduced to these modes of thought from the very beginning, since material arises in or close to every classroom throughout the working day. We already try to make children grasp what may happen to them if they run across a busy street without looking for oncoming traffic; we should go on to make them realize how other people's attempts to concentrate can be hampered by too much noise in the classroom, or how difficult it will be for Julia's mother to clean up her dress after David has dabbed it with paint. Every action can be seen in its context of effects on other people, and we have to make the assumption, and *keep on making it*, that their happiness is at least as important as our own.

As a matter of prudence we should try to ensure that children exercise all the forethought of which they are capable concerning their own well-being. As a matter of morality, we should try to induce them to extend this forethought to the well-being of others. During a school life of ten or more years it should not be impossible to establish in them these ways of thought. But can we honestly claim that at present we are doing our utmost to this end? Can we even be satisfied with our efforts to train children in elementary prudence? In view of the headlong rush of so many juveniles into cigarette smoking as a badge of adulthood, and of some into sexual activity without contraceptives in their middle teens, I think we must admit that we are failing.[1] But why do we not show them films of patients in the last stages of lung cancer, why not stress the connections between heavy smoking and bronchitis or diseases of the heart, why not emphasize the cost of tobacco in terms of other satisfactions that the money would buy . . . an instance of the utilitarian calculus which would serve quite well for arithmetical practice? If the teacher is a smoker, does he not owe the class an account of what the habit is costing him? There is something to be said for letting young people who think it smart to dabble in drug-taking see how an old addict

[1] M. Schofield, *The Sexual Behaviour of Young People*. 61 per cent of the sexually fully experienced girls in his sample never used contraceptives and 55 per cent of the experienced boys.

looks and hear from himself in person how he feels when he is cut off from supplies, or for bringing a children's officer into the classroom to tell teenagers of the problems and miseries of premature parenthood and the wretchedness of the unwanted children. Why do we not give in our schools clear and precise accounts of the symptoms of venereal diseases? Why do we not explain the commoner sequences of events leading to road accidents more often, illustrating them with police photographs of the effects; and what prevents us from giving detailed descriptions of the many types of incapacitating accident which can occur in the home itself through carelessness in cooking or home decorating or handling electrical apparatus? Finally, could we not in general science lessons give some account of various types of industrial accident which would be less likely to happen if workers had a better understanding of the risks that they were taking?[1]

The principle to be expounded is that foolhardiness is not a sign of manliness, as so many young people believe. And for those who think that life is tame unless lived dangerously, it is vital that they learn not to involve other people in their escapades. In schools of mountaineering we are first taught the safety rules, and no reputable climber would willingly endanger his companions' lives. During the early days of September 1966 a series of articles in the leading French newspaper *Figaro* discussed the immorality of the conduct of two German climbers who, having undertaken an ascent obviously beyond their powers on the Aiguille du Dru, got into difficulties from which they were unable to extricate themselves, and thereby imperilled the lives of Chamonix guides who were bound by Alpine mountaineering tradition to try to rescue them. One German was inexperienced, and the other, who was more experienced, had not done enough climbing in the current season to bring him into adequate condition for this notoriously dangerous ascent, which is only just on the verge of possibility for the climbing techniques of the day. These men, argued the writer in *Figaro*, had taken an unjustifiable risk which, if it failed, would inevitably involve the further risks of a difficult rescue. In fact one would-be rescuer lost his life. Both *Figaro* and

---

[1] *Report on Industrial Accidents*, April 1967.

the Chamonix guides treated this incident as one in which individual imprudence necessarily affecting others raises a moral issue.
The worst recent piece of collective imprudence amounting to
immoral risk-taking with the lives and well-being of others in
Britain has undoubtedly been the failure of National Coal Board
officials to make proper provision for the dumping and control of
waste from the pits of Aberfan. Nobody gave serious thought to
the situation which was allowed to develop there over several years,
and the outcome was that 166 people were killed. These instances
occurred while I was planning this book, and I quote them as
specimens for class discussion among teenagers. Any teacher who is
on the alert will similarly find current examples of imprudence and
unethical risk quoted in the newspapers or on television programmes. Discussions of such incidents are necessary to bring home
to young people that everyone has some responsibility to others for
the effects of what he does.

I have spoken of the role of the teacher as moral leader. In
every school there are other moral leaders among the pupils themselves – the boys and girls who attain outstanding positions as
head boy or girl, captains and stars of sports teams. These are the
ones most likely to impress younger children as admirable, and so
worthy of imitation. Admittedly today's cult of the pop star must
have reduced the impact of such boys and girls on their juniors in
school; nevertheless they retain the advantage of being physically
present, to be seen every day and even spoken with, a more
satisfying diet for a juvenile hero-worshipper than shadows thrown
on a screen or figures on a distant platform. But there is no doubt
that the publicity build-up of a pop star *seems* to provide more
concrete detail for the imaginations of his worshippers to play
with; here once again we meet with the substitution of fiction for
direct experience. One would rather see youngsters develop their
crushes on actual individuals who project less of a public *persona*.
Naturally the boy or girl who cuts an important figure at school is
already capable of projecting something of a public personality,
but is still much nearer than the pop star to being an ordinary
flesh and blood being who can be known, admired and imitated
as such. This situation is well appreciated by the staff of many
schools, some of whom will want to cut the school hero down to

size, while others prefer even to inflate him a little as a useful model. There is nothing disturbing in the tendency of youngsters approaching adolescence to have crushes on more or less arbitrarily chosen idols; for many people it is an important stage in emotional development and so long as the model is not given to antisocial behaviour, the resulting internalization of new standards is an invaluable piece of learning. For my own part I cannot be too grateful to that confident sixth former at my own school who lived for music with such zest and spread her views with such conviction that it never occurred to me to doubt that a plodding approach would some day bring its reward even to myself in the shape of tremendous joys in the concert hall. She literally evoked in me the belief in music, although it took many years to mature into a reliable capacity for enjoyment. Morally, it was this same eighteen-year-old who infected me with the view that only the best is good enough, and that the best in any field costs all the effort of which we are capable. Before I took on her standards my school reports were never free of indignant comment on my carelessness and untidiness; within six months her example evoked in me an obsessive neatness and a desire to get things right. This sort of emotional adventure must befall many impressionable adolescents and seems to be evidence in favour of a vertical organization of school into houses in which members from different age groups collaborate wherever possible, rather than the horizontal organization into years which must tend to isolate the younger ones from their natural models. In a school including all age groups from eleven or twelve to eighteen and nineteen, the Lower Sixth can be an excellent instrument of social and moral training, its members during that less hard driven year immediately following 'O' levels organizing and leading the athletic, cultural and social life of the entire school. Piling up of too many responsibilities on the shoulders of a few capable or over-eager teenagers unfortunately does happen in both grammar and secondary modern schools. Those who are already struggling academically in the latter type of school tend to feel that too much is expected of them by the staff when school plays and school choir are being arranged yet the staff retort that these same youngsters would be outraged if they were not given the opportunity to show their paces.

Unfortunately on occasion teachers have been known to exhibit no better sense of proportion than their charges and this does seem an area of school activities where more care might be exercised. Can we seriously expect seventeen year olds to judge how much they can undertake without detriment to some if not all of their responsibilities? Some UCCA forms make sad reading. But concentration of post-'O' level studies in Sixth Form Colleges would kill the leadership function of the sixth, removing their openings for taking responsibility and depriving the rest of the schools concerned of their natural models, roles for which fifteen and even sixteen year olds may be a little unripe.

What can we do in school to encourage the desire for genuine friendships, and to equip young people to make and maintain them, so lessening the horrors of rootlessness in our society? To begin with we should wherever possible aim at replacing rivalry with co-operation. This aim is already pretty widely accepted by teachers. We set younger children to work in groups co-operating to solve a problem. In some schools staff refrain as far as possible from assigning marks for work. The old system of going up a place or down a place in the order of the class is generally discredited. Children working together on projects may earn credit for their group instead of for themselves individually. In English lessons, where human problems are discussed, we might also lay stress on the dynamics of friendly relationships, the need for mutual forbearance and for loyal commitment.

But friendship will always be difficult to achieve where the level of communication is low. Opportunities for misunderstanding proliferate when people do not know how to convey to each other their feelings or views with any degree of precision.[1] The supremely important use of the technique of oracy therefore lies in the promotion of friendship.

Oracy is probably more commonly treated as a first step towards *literacy* in the children of under-privileged environments. They are stimulated to tell, instead of write, about their experiences. The

---

[1] Precise communication is difficult without the use of abstract expressions such as some working class families are quite unacquainted with. cf. Basil Bernstein, 'Social Structure, Language and Learning' in *Educational Research*, Vol. III, no. 3, pp. 163–76.

teacher lays on the opportunity for a new experience, the child reacts and then talks about it to the teacher or the group. So new words are learned as the need to use them is felt. As vocabulary grows, so also does the power to make distinctions within the child's own stream of awareness, to note for instance, that this is of a redder tone of yellow than that, more like the peel of an orange than that of a lemon; that this is harder, lasts longer, makes a more high-pitched sound when struck; progressing eventually to an expressed perception of subtle differences such as that between the colour of the same thing when it is in sunlight and when it is in shadow, or between how we feel on a crisp frosty morning and how we feel on a warm damp one. Many people from poorer homes do badly in academic work because they are unused to putting anything into words, and without the use of words as indices of differences perceived, we *cannot* think much beyond the level of intelligent apes. Nor can the home with a small vocabulary (where the family communicate little except their basic appetites and desires) prepare children for friendship involving mutual understanding. Naturally this applies to the more developed aspects of married life. People will not be able to understand grievances which they themselves cannot express, and these can easily become cancerous growths within a relationship. We come to understand other people, and ourselves, through talking around our difficulties and so exploring them. Therefore to fulfil themselves children must enjoy the use of words in their companionships as well as in their thinking.

They have also to learn how to listen to what other people say, to digest it by relating it to what is already familiar, and to repeat it accurately instead of immediately transforming it into whatever they themselves expected or wanted to hear. They have to learn to *act* on information received from others, and to act in a manner genuinely appropriate to what they have been told. Bearing all this in mind, it becomes obvious that class discussions require the firmest leadership from the teacher in charge, who must strive to prevent the development of misunderstandings. It is only thus that communication can become truly educational as well as pleasurable. It should be grasped that talk has a great variety of functions besides that of conveying information. We talk in order to give outlets to our feelings of love, aggression or frustration, or even to act out in conversation some part that we cannot directly play in action (as lecherous talk is a substitute for making love, or boasting a substitute for outdoing our rivals). Talk can also be ritual, as in conventional greetings or ceremonies. It can be used to request, plead, command, or declare intentions. All of its many functions need to be called into use between people if they are to communicate fully with one another. And only the fullest communication will make social life worth living and enable people to make roots quickly after moving into a new environment. American loquacity plainly has the function of bringing newcomers quickly into touch with one another in a country where geographical mobility has always been high. In England we find the nearest counterpart to American sociability in the life of remote country districts where practically everybody joins in at fairs, gymkhanas, school concerts, jumble sales and meetings of local clubs. A genuinely sociable person has no difficulty in getting to know others quite well in such areas, whereas in most of our towns and suburbs it is not nearly so easy. In our own countryside, just as in the U.S.A., the power to talk readily to strangers is an important factor in well-being; we should aim at extending this habit to our towns, where people continue to meet freely in shopping centres, parks and cafés.

Thus in school we could be preparing children to avoid becoming entirely rootless, however often they may have to move house. We can present friendly relationships as a goal in life; we can promote conversational fluency as a means towards making contact with others, and improve the effectiveness of communication by training children to express themselves more exactly and listen more carefully.

At the present day religious instruction is probably the least satisfactory subject on the syllabus for both teachers and pupils. With the decline in formalized religious belief, numbers of teachers would prefer not to undertake religious instruction at all. To have to attempt it without either conviction or specialized knowledge is frustrating; uncertainty or cynicism tends to get across unintentionally.

But what happens if we abandon religious instruction in

schools? The first and most obvious effect is the loss to children of an important part of their cultural heritage, biblical stories from both testaments. Many of these may not be regarded as especially meaningful in themselves, yet if they are not part of the furniture of one's mind, how is one to make sense of the innumerable literary and artistic references to them from the Middle Ages onwards? How far is one to absorb the religious feeling of Giovanni Bellini's madonnas, or of the crucifixions of Flemish painting? Without knowledge of the story of Jesus Christ the tenderest madonna is seen and felt only as a mother-and-child study, lacking the deeper poignancy that arises from contemplating it with the fate of Jesus in mind. Similarly if we do not know why Jesus was crucified and how He was resurrected, even the most moving crucifixion in art begins to take on something of the crudity of a horror comic. A great cathedral is not merely an architectural achievement, it is a temple. The more we know about how God is worshipped within it, the better we can appreciate it as a building. When biblical incidents and characters are mentioned by writers, we lose much of the force of the reference if we have first had to look it up like an archaic expression in Chaucer; it was intended to strike home immediately, to evoke an echo in a Christian mind. The parables of the talents and the mustard seed, the concept of the kingdom of heaven, are such as should become familiar when we are young so that they can receive illumination from our experiences and in turn illuminate them. The story of Jesus Christ should be known to everyone, not merely as history, but as material to be pondered over and seen in the context of ordinary lives. Even for people who are not Christians, Jesus is not just a character in an ancient political squabble; He is a great symbolic figure whose story can be interpreted in many ways. It is impossible to contemplate it without becoming profoundly involved in it. The crucifixion points to the underlying tragedy of the human condition.

But religious teaching need not be confined to Christian texts and doctrines. Many schools have found it worth while to give instruction on Hinduism, Buddhism and Islam, and to promote reading of selected passages from their scriptures.

It can be argued that any enquiry into the fundamental nature and the purpose of human life is religious in character. But this sort of philosophical enterprise is only suitable for those who show spontaneous interest in it during their latter years in school. It would probably need to be conducted by specialists with some qualifications in philosophy, since no untrained person can be relied on to present all the arguments and their implications. It is important not to encourage one-sided views before the alternatives have been studied.

Without a concept of the existence of something beyond and greater than ourselves, human life loses in depth and significance, as anyone who alternates between atheism and any form of theism will testify. Human beings deeply need to feel respect or awe for the universe to which they belong, for this is the source of our respect for our fellow beings and for what is most fundamental in ourselves. Without it life tends to be a shallow business of battening and being battened on. There is also in the religious attitude a feeling for permanence, something we very much need in the rootless urban society of today. Boys and girls need to feel that although individuals come and go, the order of nature persists (perhaps as some sort of super-person?) in which nothing that ever has been is completely lost. The individual is small and transient, but he is also unique with great possibilities for development – an irreplaceable element in that whole which gives to individuals their meaning. The contemporary Way of Fragmentation, which presents individuals as warring self-contained units, is a way of loss. It is in those phases during which we lose all feeling of belonging to a fellowship of sentient beings that we suffer most cruelly. The extreme case of this is the schizophrenic. Many people feel today that some version of pantheism is more widely acceptable than Christianity in the context of modern knowledge, because pantheism emphasizes that all individuals are part of one Whole.

Allowing that all the same a knowledge of Christianity needs to be imparted for its significance in our cultural heritage and that somehow a religious attitude needs to be inculcated, we still have to deal with the problem of the official attitude of the school to Christian doctrine. Can we make use of Christian prayers, hymns and forms of speech in school assembly while at the same time in the classroom we treat them as open to question? In practice it is the headmaster who decides. Some have found acceptable and meaningful ways of building school assembly around ethical and philosophical ideas. But is it entirely satisfactory to leave this to the judgement of individual headmasters? A headmaster lacking in religious feeling may leave his school without an effective lead in these matters. Perhaps school assembly should always be taken by a believer. We cannot let children go away with the impression that religious belief makes no difference to anyone's life. It is important that there should be no feeling of duplicity, where a formal and hypocritical declaration of Christian faith at the official level is accompanied by a cold scepticism pervading school activities.

I have been discussing aesthetic, moral and religious education as counter-vailing influences to the various pressures exerted by modern urbanized society on our young people. Today's urbanized society tends in all ways to blunt sensibility and to impose a uniform way of life that limits the individual's power and wish to develop constructively as far as he is able. Aesthetic and religious education should revitalize the towndweller, while moral education puts him in the way of improving other people's chances of happiness as well as his own.

VI · The Changing Role of Women and its Educational Implications

Another social change which has been proceeding at an ever-increasing pace is the inter-related sexual and economic emancipation of women. From the time when they leave school girls now command higher wages in relation to boys' and even adults' than they used to do, commonly keep a higher proportion of their earnings for themselves than was customary before the war, and have a far wider range of occupations. The effect of these changes has been to increase the self confidence of women and their potential independence of fathers, lovers and husbands. My husband and I in *The Permissive Morality* argued that this has contributed to the current free and easy attitude to sexual behaviour, since the girl who can pay her way in the world has little to fear from father or mother and so may consider herself at liberty to do as she thinks fit in her sexual relationships.[1] It is not so much that girls flaunt their intimacies with boys in the faces of their parents (rather they tend to maintain a discreet silence, leaving their parents to wonder what is going on), as that they believe and say that how they conduct their love affairs is their own business and in this parents seem to acquiesce. Usually they feel that they have no choice but to acquiesce.

The unchaperoned party at home and the privacy afforded by their own transport facilities give boys and girls many opportunities for heavy petting or even intercourse. Schofield's study shows clearly that fairly heavy petting is common among those who have reached the age of eighteen.[2] 38 per cent of his sample of teenage girls would not agree that premarital intercourse was wrong; 13 per cent of nineteen year old girls actually admitted to being fully sexually experienced. Schofield found that grammar school girls interviewed tended to break off at the medium petting

[1] C. H. and W. M. Whiteley, *The Permissive Morality*, pp. 29–30.
[2] M. Schofield, *The Sexual Behaviour of Young People*.

66

stage, whereas advanced petting and full intercourse were commoner among secondary modern and comprehensive girls. (One
is, of course, at liberty to suspect that the latter might have been
more candid in interview than the former. Schofield admits that
some of his interviewers got such different results from others
that it is likely that the actual incidence of premarital intercourse
among teenage girls is somewhat higher than his complete figures
suggest.) It is possible to panic at these findings, seeing the open
admissions to intercourse and heavy petting as a relatively small
proportion of actual sexual experience among teenagers, but some
people go to the other extreme and are astonished when girls who
to them have seemed innocent turn out to be pregnant. The truth
is that we do not know for certain the extent of full sexual experience among schoolchildren, any more than that of other age
groups. Schofield's figures may be taken as a minimum. His
results do not point to much promiscuity among the girls since
the experienced ones averaged only two partners apiece (although
here again we must take into account that those already married,
and the most promiscuous girls who were in care, in prison or
attending V.D. clinics when interviewed, are excluded from this
sample). The picture he reveals is of a relatively small group of
teenage wantons who between them cater for the sexual needs of
large numbers of boys, while six out of seven girls in the sample
remain technically virgin at nineteen and the seventh usually
makes love only with the boy with whom she is going steady. Mary
Morse's social worker in Northtown among coffee-bar habitués
'gathered from their conversation that sexual intercourse was
accepted as a matter of course quite early on in any relationship'.[1]

We cannot say for certain that the situation is different from
that of fifty years ago because no comparable figures exist. But
fifty years ago it is unlikely that any such survey as Schofield's
could have been made at all; most young people would have been
too scared of admitting to any sexual behaviour beyond the mildest
kissing and cuddling, and it is certain that parents, teachers and
clergymen would have banded together to put a stop to the
investigation as soon as they found out that such questions were
being asked. Today we discuss sex altogether more openly,

[1] M. Morse, *The Unattached*, p. 116.

information is freely available, and even quite respectable works of fiction may include detailed descriptions of intercourse (e.g. J. G. Cozzens, *By Love Possessed*; A. Sharp, *A Green Tree in Gedde*), and the sexually provocative nature of some mass entertainment and advertisements has long been matter for comment. With so much more now said and written about sex, and so many more opportunities than their predecessors ever had, it really would be surprising if girls today were not far more sexually experienced than girls used to be. The most alarming feature of the situation is the irresponsibility of those who go in for intercourse without using contraceptives while they are still too young to settle to married life or child rearing, and probably cannot afford either to furnish a home or to bring up a baby. 61 per cent of the sexually experienced girls in Schofield's sample admitted that they never used birth control devices. If we suppose that they left the responsibility for contraception to the boys we get no comfort there, for 55 per cent of the experienced boys said they did not regularly attempt birth control, half of them either because they did not like contraceptives or simply did not care. (There is reason to believe that the risk itself is part of the attraction of intercourse for very young people.) In any case many of the early experiences seem to have been unpremeditated, when circumstances happened to be propitious.

Older people tend to forget, if they ever knew it, that when one is young there is a heady excitement in having intercourse, not merely for the pleasure or physical satisfaction involved, but as a gesture of self assertion. So the number of births of illegitimate children to teenage girls increases yearly, together with the number of marriages in which the bride is under twenty-one.[1] But the percentage of marriages ending in divorce is much higher in these younger age groups and it therefore seems reasonable to suppose that few teenagers are mature enough for marriage and that marriage when the girl becomes pregnant is not often a sound solution. Effective contraceptive practice is all-important among the young unmarried, whatever their attitude to it may be, so that

[1] Schofield points out that illegitimate births to girls under twenty as a percentage of all such births have risen from 17·2 per cent in 1950 to 20·5 per cent in 1962.

they will neither bring into the world babies they do not seriously want and cannot properly provide for, nor rush into marriage partnerships that have small chance of working out well.

It seems likely that a great deal could be done in schools to improve this situation. According to Schofield schools give altogether more sex education to girls than to boys. But what form does it take? I have come across a school where an unmarried Roman Catholic woman biology teacher had sole responsibility for the girls' sex education, which consisted of little more than a bald account of the nature and functioning of the reproductive organs, as though human beings differed little in their sex life from cattle or monkeys. But boys and girls require much more information than this barnyard stuff. In particular they need to know how the sexes differ in their approach to mating, how fatally easy it is, for instance, for the girl to become emotionally involved just as her boyfriend, liberated from his physical urgency, is ready to say goodbye to her. Boys should be told that it is the nature of girls to be clinging and that it is unfair to them to treat them cavalierly. Girls should be made aware of the strength of sexual desire in boys, of their high potency in their teens, and therefore of the cruelty and the danger of leading them on without intending to satisfy them. No girl should leave school unaware that in sexual intimacy with a boy it is she who is taking all the risks, physically and emotionally, for a one-in-three chance of pleasure (Schofield), and that sympathy for a desirous boy can be an expensive feeling to give in to – the reasonable reply to 'You would if you loved me' being 'You wouldn't ask me if you loved *me*' (One in three sexually experienced girls becomes pregnant. Schofield). Both boys and girls should be encouraged to see that treating others as mere instruments of pleasure or excitement is unjustifiable, and that sexual relationships ought to be something other than episodes in a war between male and female. Thus the psychology of the sexes and the sound utilitarian reasons for self control (or, if self control is too difficult, efficient birth control) should be taught during the later years of secondary education, probably not later than thirteen. The simple biology of the subject is appropriate to much younger classes in the junior schools, since girls may begin to menstruate before leaving junior school. The risks of catching a venereal disease from strangers and the nature of these diseases also urgently need to be made known, since so many 'early starters' in sex are initiated by people they hardly know (Schofield). Few of Schofield's interviewees would have been able to recognize the symptoms of the diseases – a dangerous situation. His team found boys and girls usually keen enough to discuss all aspects of sex, though not, they said, with unmarried teachers who cannot claim to speak out of a complete experience. It is obvious that whoever undertakes schools sex education of young people should have some sympathy for their points of view and be liked and trusted by them, yet be capable of taking a firm line. Some people argue that sex education should be left to the parents, but unfortunately large numbers of parents are either unwilling or incompetent sex instructors, and some parents will object to this sort of instruction being given at all. I think the answer is that where the parents are willing and able to chaperone their daughters as Muslim parents do (but hardly anyone else) the objection may be upheld; otherwise not.

The question of how effectively the school itself is able to chaperone its own pupils is increasingly important now that many schools are changing over from single sex to mixed. Too many incidents occur of boys engaging in sex play with girls or even raping them in unsupervised classrooms, outdoor sheds, laboratories or gymnasiums. For instance, at a Nuneaton juvenile court in June 1967 two fifteen-year old girls were said to have had sexual intercourse with boys in a biology classroom while teachers were marking G.C.E. papers in another room. These girls admitted having had intercourse on thirty-eight occasions in eighteen months in a derelict house and other places. One of them, apologizing in court to the Headmaster for her behaviour, said, 'I want you to know that we were not the only ones. We wanted to tell you really, but couldn't.' The solicitor representing the school pointed out that only two of the incidents took place in the school, both in places that were normally supervised. However, this surely shows that boys and girls can never be left unsupervised in school, even for fifteen minutes, which in this case was quite long enough for intercourse to take place, and that rooms may need to be kept locked when they are not being used. I have heard of other similar incidents which never reached the newspapers, including a series on the premises of a mixed selective secondary school in the 1920s. In schools where such things happen, curiosity is inevitably aroused among other children as to what the experience is like. Since it is impossible to prevent them from seeing, hearing and reading sexually stimulating material at every turn, it is only reasonable to arm young people with the fullest possible knowledge and understanding of the risks they run in joining in sex games before they are ready for marriage.

Teachers and others who wonder how the youthful experimenters with sex can be identified may be interested to know that among girls there is a very high positive correlation between smoking twenty or more cigarettes a day and being sexually fully experienced (Schofield). Both the smoking and the sexual intercourse are self-indulgent, careless of consequences, and can be represented as assertions of adulthood and of defiance of parents. (Girls who got on well with their mothers in Schofield's sample generally refrained from intercourse.) There were twice as many girls with plenty of pocket money among the experienced as among the inexperienced. The more sexually experienced a boy was, the more jobs he was likely to have had. The picture which emerges is of a teenage society in which those with most to spend are the most restless and self-indulgent, and these are the ones most given to premarital sexual experiment, the boys to begin with often relying on casual encounters with older girls, the girls initiated by older boys with whom they tend to have long lasting relationships. Their sex behaviour depends, however, very much on the facilities available. Those who meet on commercial premises are more likely to be experienced than those who meet at home or in youth clubs.

Teachers who are distressed by these revelations may be cheered to read that Burgess and Wallis in 1953 found that 90 per cent of women who had had premarital intercourse said that it had strengthened their marital relationship. We must hope that today's sexually experienced girls will be able to say the same. Most of Schofield's sample, including those who were fully experienced, disapproved of adultery. But I think it is clear that girls and boys should leave school understanding what is involved in sexual relationships, and prepared to think of the consequences of what they do. It is important to evoke in them a vivid conviction of the selfishness of sexual exploitation, and the absolute wrong of producing unwanted babies. When youngsters appear callous, it is often because their imaginations have not been touched.

Their greater awareness of sexual possibilities and their claim to regulate their own sex life before they marry, form only one aspect of the changing role of women in English society today. Another aspect, which likewise is an effect of their economic emancipation, is their growing tendency to go out to work after they are married. It is now quite normal for a newly married girl to continue with her job until she becomes pregnant and her earnings help to make up the payments on the home and its furnishings. The reality of the partnership between the couple becomes more obvious when each shares in the provision of the home, and many wives return to work as soon as their children are going to school, some even earlier, leaving their little ones with a grandmother or other relative, or a child-minder if no nursery school can take them. The reasons for this are not always purely economic. Many women dislike housework and would sooner relegate it to evenings and weekends when they may be able to share some of it out between children and husband. Others find domestic work very lonely, for the companionship of young children can be boring. The plain truth is that what is traditionally women's work does not appeal to all of them. Nor is it always possible for them to discover beforehand how they will react to year after year of housewifery and childcare. Many a woman has found to her horror that the baby in her arms is after all an unwelcome stranger; to go out to work is in such cases a great relief. Then there are those who, even though they enjoy motherhood, fail to find in it the fulfilment or justification they seek in life, and have to convince themselves through some outside commitment that they are not merely domestic serfs. The insistence on equal partnership with the husband, both earning for the family and both taking part in the care of the home, has become a phenomenon of postwar life, more common among the working classes than among the middle classes, and may well have derived some impetus from that wartime period when all women without young children were conscripted and sent to work in factories, offices and shops.[1]

The social effects of this development are complex and vary greatly from one family to another. Obviously there will be more money, often for luxuries such as a more expensive washing machine or refrigerator, holidays abroad, a car, or even a second car. But this gain has to be offset by the loss of the wife as home maker and home tender during most of each day. How can the home be so well looked after if she is not there to work in it? A childless couple living in a flat may find no such disadvantage in the wife's going out to work, but a family in a house with children rushing in and out from garden and street in all weathers can almost always look as though it needs a thorough scouring when the mother goes out regularly to work. Intelligent organization and the co-operation of the entire family will be required to keep such a home well-ordered and reasonably clean, and it is safe to surmise that not too many households meet these requirements. So while their living standard has risen, in the sense that they can now afford to eat steak instead of sausage, that they have a car, an automatic washing machine and the latest model of television set, it has fallen in the sense that father regularly runs out of clean socks, his loose buttons are not sewn on unless he has learned to do it for himself, the kitchen is so messy that the family have far more gastric upsets and, as one such father gaily remarked to me, 'If anything got clean, we should take it to the pawnshop!' Gracious living is out. Nobody would have time for it. To this we must add the irritability of the overworked wife who cannot keep up with the claims on her attention. In such a situation children may begin to feel that they are not appreciated, and those approaching adolescence may seek comfort in precocious love affairs, or simply express their sense of injury by getting into trouble. The woman's own life may suffer from overstrain, but on the other hand, she may benefit from the sheer interest of her outside job and her respite from lonely brooding (housework done day after day in isolation gives some housewives unrivalled opportunities for hatching grievances or anxieties), or else she may find

---

[1] cf. J. and E. Newson, *Infant Care in an Urban Community*.

6

herself evenly balanced between overstrain and the relief from neurotic apathy provided by an outside interest.

Morally, the family of the working housewife stands to lose in at least three ways. Being short of time and vitality for keeping them up to scratch on cleanliness, punctuality, honesty and so on, she may let their standards slide, or else confuse them by sometimes insisting on getting things right and at other times just giving up. So the children get accustomed to an unthinking impulsive permissiveness – bad training for them as future parents who must in their turn set standards, although some children will react with a strictness of their own. Secondly, contributing her share to the material well-being of the family, she may come to think that she has as good a right as her husband to the occasional sexual fling, which leaves her at a disadvantage when insisting on chastity in her children. Thirdly, emphasis may have been put too firmly on the value of material acquisition at the expense of leisure for aesthetic or intellectual pursuits, or just for orderly living. Children tend to accept the values expressed by their parents in what they actually do rather than in anything they say. An overworked woman dripping cigarette ash into the washing-up bowl, and cleaning the living room on the one day of the week when the family can all be at home together, just so that they may afford a bigger television set and car than the ones next door, is teaching her family that the most important thing in life is being able to buy more ostentatiously than your acquaintances.

Despite these disadvantages to family life, it is certain that society's need for married women to work outside their homes is going to increase rather than decline in the years ahead. For there are now fewer girls reared than boys, fewer of these girls remain single, and most marry earlier and have children earlier, so that their labour is removed from the market before they have had time to attain professional maturity and when they eventually return they need a refresher course before they can be really useful. So the shortage of skilled women workers such as teachers and nurses, already troublesome, must inevitably grow to crisis point. We shall be obliged to instal crèches in schools and hospitals for the children of staff, and to multiply our day nurseries. Even when we have done all this women workers will go on being in short supply and more and more will be expected from them; but because women are as they are, most of them will try to respond to the demands made on them. They may get better pay than before but are sure to get heavier workloads. When teachers for instance are in short supply, those available do not do less work, but more. Of course more men will have to go into nursing and teaching to replace some of the missing women.

Reflection shows that boys are going to have to be trained very differently from the way they used to be and often still are, because many will be confronted with an entirely different role in life. The old ideal of the Manly Man who would not know how to change the baby's nappy and would not think of washing up, much less of carrying bed-pans in a hospital ward or watching over five year olds with their Cuisenaire rods in a classroom, will soon be all but obsolete, and mothers and teachers who adhere to it are doing a disservice to their boys by delaying a necessary adjustment. Boys as well as girls as a matter of course will need to learn plain cooking, sewing repairs, how to clean out a room, and how to shop economically in the supermarkets. They will have to share the girls' lessons on child care and the growth of little children. They will be faced with the prospect not only of taking mixed classes in secondary schools but of teaching very small children. Nursing in mens' wards of hospitals will ultimately be done by men only. Once the last of the great army of spinsters, who have hitherto been the staple of our teaching and nursing staffs, reaches retirement the situation will rapidly alter in this direction. The old strict division of work into men's jobs and women's will break down. Perhaps eventually women will cease altogether being shut unwillingly into small nuclear households to become neurotic and socially useless; their husbands and children will come to accept that *they* too have their share to do of the housework, which will become a common task when both husband and wife go out to work.

For any such revolution to proceed painlessly, boys must be trained not only to undertake domestic tasks but to give up their cherished belief that men are more important than women, that if sacrifices in convenience and leisure have to be made the women must make them all. The scaling-down of hours of work that we are promised as automation extends its province will give many men more spare time than their wives, and boys should be brought up to believe that a woman needs as much time for recuperation and amusement as a man. If their mothers will not try at home to prevent English boys from perpetuating the old irrational male superiority complex, teachers will have to do it instead. Co-education of the sexes indeed accustoms boys and girls to one another's society, so that neither sex is any longer a mystery to the other at the level of work and social life. But care will need to be taken in co-educational schools to prevent boys from assuming as their right all the commanding positions in pupils' own school activities, chairmanships of societies and so on. Some girls still today have a marked inferiority complex in the presence of boys with whom they are pursuing any activity, except those centred on courtship and child care. The tradition of the superior intellectual and organizing abilities of the male is very tough and until girls have been pressed into showing their paces and encouraged to stand up to masculine scorn and mistrust, we shall not know for sure whether the female tendency to take a back seat in mixed company has much real justification in higher male competence. Even if it has, the girls need to be manœuvred into showing more spirit and undertaking responsibilities that they now shirk. Both boys and girls need to accept the view that a girl attempting a job of organizing or representing fellow pupils in a mixed school is not a figure of fun. The biological role of girls is admittedly more passive than that of boys, and girls are inferior to boys in muscular strength, but we live in a society in which muscular strength is steadily becoming less important and female passivity is being called into question. In every large mixed group there are likely to be girls who are more clever and enterprising than many of the boys; it is important that these girls should be given the corresponding opportunities and that everyone should see this as natural. The lesson to be learned is that men and women are to be partners in life, not rivals, nor set in the attitudes of leaders and led respectively. What counts in the individual is not his sex but his particular abilities and his manner of using them. Boys are more aggressive, more self-assertive than girls and so boys press their claims to the more interesting tasks which earn credit and acclaim, leaving to girls the more onerous and tedious jobs. But if the relative roles of the sexes in our society are changing, so that both must take a share in domestic work and both must go out to work, boys will have to learn to accept more than they now do of that which is onerous and dull in life and girls must learn to take more responsibility and show more initiative.

It is the need to show herself especially suitable for a professional undertaking that makes the 'career girl' subtly or openly self assertive as compared with other girls; she has to be that bit better than her male competitors before she will be considered for the opening at all and she soon comes to know this. If she does succeed, her personality is likely to have been submitted to unnecessary strains and to be none the better for the experience. Surely we have reached the point in history at which we should be leaving this state of affairs behind? Yet the Newsom Report argues that we should restrict the range of subjects open to girls and treat them educationally as second class citizens. It is worth noticing also that in his *Rise of the Meritocracy* Michael Young assumes without argument that the girls will not be included in the educational rat race of the future and so will become the natural leaders in the ultimate revolt of the rejected, the non-academic masses.[1] The new back-to-the-kitchen movement which seeks to cut short the full education of girls on the grounds that when they have been trained most of them will have to take time off for childbearing, and are therefore not worth training, is fairly strong today and likely to become stronger when the present generation of spinsters retires from influential positions in the field of education. Until the logic of the dire shortage of good quality teachers and Heads compels the 'back-to-the-kitchen' school to confess that there just are not enough male candidates of the right calibre to fill the gap, we shall very likely have years of pretending that it is in the interest of society to economize on higher education for girls. The whole of English society, and the educational world in particular, will be the worse off for this trend. I hope that teachers of both boys and girls will realize the danger of letting it grow unchecked. The way out of the female Motherhood-versus-Job dilemma is not to imprison our girls in the nuclear family home,

[1] M. Young; *Rise of the Meritocracy*.

but to go ahead with the provision of crèches attached to work-places, and more nursery schools. For it is not only the child who stands to benefit from nursery school experience; the mothers themselves, and society at large, both need the earlier liberation of wives from day-in-day-out servitude to the requirements of infants. Public opinion on this topic could be mobilized through discussions among older schoolchildren and the deliberate training of girls to take their full share of undomestic activities. We did not discover how many kinds of work women could efficiently do until the labour shortages of the two World Wars compelled us to substitute women workers for men. Similarly I doubt whether we shall discover either the organizing abilities of many women or the talent of many men for teaching small children until we are willing to employ women more widely as organizers and administrators, and men more widely as primary school teachers. It is the old question of giving people the work they are best fitted to do by temperament and ability. Anyone who still believes that all women are cast in much the same tem-peramental mould of passivity, docility, instability and depen-dence, and all men in the same mould of enterprise, aggressiveness and steadiness should bear in mind that there have existed societies such as the Arapesh where both sexes were trained for the same parental role of tending the young, the Mundugumor where both sexes were brought up to be turbulent and gay, the Tchambuli whose men were temperamental and irresponsible while their wives co-operated cheerfully in the work of the community.[1] We need by experiment to find out the facts concerning the relative capacities of individuals instead of burying our heads in the sands of tradition. What is rather troubling at present is the suspicion that as we change over from single sex schools to mixed schools, fewer of the girls will get the opportunity to find out whether they have any organizing ability at all, or any power of leadership.

Thus on many counts, helping young people who are still at school to adjust to the changing roles of men and women may turn out to be among the most important things we can hope to do.

[1] Margaret Mead; *Sex and Temperament in Three Primitive Societies.*

VII · Coloured Immigrants in Schools

Another area of social change that I would like to discuss is the recent influx of coloured immigrants into urban districts, an influx that is still being supplemented by the arrival of their children and to some degree by illicit immigration. The problems presented in numbers of city schools by some of the coloured children are already acute, and with the inevitable dispersal of coloured families throughout the towns many more schools are going to be affected. Although I have seen admirable studies of the problem of giving adequate instruction in English as a second language to the young immigrants, I have nowhere found an account of the behaviour difficulties presented by some of them in the classroom. Yet to refuse to discuss these is unrealistic. It is important to get as clear and unbiased a view as possible of what is happening, so that the difficulties can be tackled sympathetically and effectively instead of being swept under the rug as at present, or viewed with prejudice. Teachers and teacher trainees as well as social workers need up-to-date information about the home and cultural backgrounds of the newcomers, and the problems they are likely to raise. For this purpose we ought to have textbooks based on research into the family structure, behaviour and changing attitudes of the various immigrant groups. A number of these have already been done on West Indians and Katrin Fitzherbert's admirably written 'West Indian Children in London' provides a useful summary leading up to her account of her own research into the problems of taking West Indian children 'into care' in a London borough. I found her account of West Indian life matched exactly what I had seen for myself and heard from teaching staff in Birmingham schools with well over $33\frac{1}{3}$ per cent of coloured children. The cultural and family backgrounds of Asiatics are better known and more easily grasped. I shall myself try to give in a brief statement the main characteristics of the more exotic immigrant groups and the general patterns of behaviour of their children in our schools. My information on their ways of life in England has been checked with the Welfare Liaison Officer for the Commonwealth Welfare Council to the West Midlands, Mr T. G. Ayre, who is himself engaged on research into the family structures and attitudes of the coloured in his district. My purpose is to make some contribution towards the understanding of an intricate situation, and discuss ways of coping fairly and effectively with it in schools.

It is disappointing to find the Plowden committee writing as though the only educational difficulties raised by coloured immi-grant children were linguistic, apart from 'the embarrassing eagerness' of some of them 'for the disciplined booklearning and formal instruction of their own culture . . . when the language diffi-culty prevents the school explaining fully to parents the different way we go about education in England' (paragraph 183). It must be the Asiatic children who are thus spoken of as eager for the formal instruction of their own culture – many of those who have mastered English prove to be diligent scholars – and one can well understand the bewilderment of their parents when we try to explain to them in words they can understand the informal methods now current in many of our schools. For we are in the midst of an educational revolution such as they never dreamed of and their offspring are caught up in it willy nilly. They still expect their children to be learning by rote. Some even appear to believe that exposure to a given educative course will magically alter the child's state of knowledge without his making any par-ticipatory effort; if he has been physically present at the course they think that he should automatically be regarded as qualified thereby and in no need of examinations or tests to prove his ability. Thus from the outset parents and school are at cross purposes; a real problem. But I find it impossible to understand how the Plowden committee can have been satisfied that they had looked into the complete range of difficulties when they only mention this and the language problem.

The tide of coloured immigrants, chiefly West Indians, Indians, and Pakistanis, has been pouring into this country at an accelerat-ing rate from the early 1950s until it was (partly) stemmed by the operation of the amendment of August 1965 to the Immigration

Act of 1962. At first it consisted of men in search of jobs in a country short of labour. Many lived in 'boarding houses' run by coloured landlords, usually fairly big old-fashioned houses with attics and cellars which could accommodate numbers of single men dormitory style, and could often be bought cheaply because their leases were short. When my husband and I sold my father's Victorian house in Birmingham in 1954, most of the would-be purchasers were coloured; they examined the cellars with care, clearly regarding them as sleeping accommodation. We heard of houses in the vicinity where the beds were occupied by alternating day and night shifts and at week-ends the gardens were filled with the drying washing of the dozens of tenants. Most of these with the passing of time were able to save enough to pay the fares of their wives and families, whom they proceeded to house in so-called 'flats' consisting of one or two rooms with shared cooking and washing facilities. Such accommodation is horribly cramped in relation to the number of persons using it. A peripatetic teacher of English told me of one West Indian family whose daughter, aged fourteen, was never able to read at home in preparation for her training as a nursing assistant, because of the living conditions. The entire family shared a single room between eleven and twelve feet square, with a large double bed curtained off in one corner, chairs, a heater and a television set furnishing the remainder of the space. The table, shared between three families, was out on the landing with the cooker, and was permanently piled up with a mixture of clean and dirty crockery. Meals were eaten standing or roaming about the room and landing. The only artificial lighting was from a single hanging low-watt bulb. In such conditions no youngster could possibly do homework. The most astonishing feature of such West Indian homes is the high standard of cleanliness attained under circumstances which would break the heart of most white women. If anyone deserves to be rehoused in a new flat, surely it is a family which has shown how it can maintain its self-respect in such a dwelling. Those local authorities who house applicants in accordance with their standards of cleanliness in the homes they already have, are housing West Indian families alongside white ones, and seem fully justified in their policy. The one ground of objection that white neighbours might fairly raise against a few West Indian families is their noisiness. But surely a little consultation would take care of this difficulty, for the people who are insensitive to noise could all be housed close together. It therefore seems reasonable to attribute the covert refusal of some local authorities to house West Indian applicants in council flats or on municipal housing estates, to fear of the effects of white tenants' colour prejudice on subsequent election results. It is freely said in some places that any political party which allowed coloured tenants to occupy desirable municipal housing would find itself losing seats on the local council. The authorities concerned are unwilling to put this statement to the test, and coloured applicants on the housing register find themselves shuffled back and forth between streets shortly due for demolition.

What is perhaps most misleading about West Indians living in English towns is the fact that they claim to speak English and *be* English, whereas many speak a Creole dialect with such slovenly diction and mangled syntax that English people cannot understand what they say, especially when they are excited. Many are also totally lacking in understanding of our way of life or our moral standards, and thus many misunderstandings arise. If they were to admit to themselves that here they are as yet strangers in a strange culture to which they have still to acclimatize themselves, they would learn to fit in more quickly and easily.

What sort of background do they come from? From a sunny climate, where life can be lived for the most part out of doors. There they sleep in a small cabin with little expenditure on rent or furnishings and the change from that to expensive rented rooms in this country with heating to be paid for plus curtains, rugs and chairs before there is any comfort at all, must be a drastic one. Clothing for our climate is another unwonted expense and a technique to be learned. West Indians will, however, normally be found quite suitably attired in cold weather, with thick coats and wool-lined boottees. The vivid colours they favour have also come into fashion of late. But how much they must miss their own bright climate and the free relaxed life of their home communities, where there is nothing corresponding to our tight little nuclear family ensconced as though for a siege in its own dwelling. West Indians are used to the extended family system operating in a more free and easy style than anything that used to be current in Bethnal Green when Young and Willmott were preparing *Family and Kinship in East London*. The West Indian working class family in the Caribbean is matriarchal in structure, each daughter tending to live with her mother while she (the daughter) takes lovers and has children by them until finally she discovers a man prepared to take responsibility for her and all her brood, and to be a reliable, loving and respectful husband. This 'pattern' is carried over from Caribbean life to life in England and is a relic of the old slave system under which marriage was not for negroes, who belonged primarily to their white owners. Not surprisingly, in the West Indies the men have become irresponsible and some women never marry at all. Katrin Fitzherbert in 'West Indian Children in London' distinguishes four forms of sexual association in the West Indies. There is legal marriage, usual among middle-class West Indians who have a quasi-Victorian outlook, but seldom undertaken among the working classes until both bride and groom are mature and already have several children, some of them grown up. In the West Indies even if he wanted to marry his girl early in life the prospective groom could not afford to do it in what is considered the proper style, imitated from white settlers, with the wife staying at home instead of earning. There is also a special style of legal working class marriage associated with hellfire Christianity and contracted quite young, in which the husband is authoritarian although he may have to let his wife go out to work to help finance the household. The children of this sort of marriage are strictly raised and kept away from evil influences. Then there is the first stage on the way towards legal marriage, regular cohabitation, known as 'faithful concubinage' or 'common-law marriage', although this is not recognized in law. This is an egalitarian relationship in which both spouses earn to keep the home going. The wife may bring in stepchildren from former unions and their position in this one is variable and uninstitutionalized. The stability of a 'common-law marriage' is unreliable. In Judith Blake's sample in *Family Structure in Jamaica*, the average time such unions lasted was 3·5 years. Finally there are all the more or less irregular affairs in which the father may or may not contribute to the upkeep of the children. West Indian women 'think they stand a better chance of getting help from a man if they remain on good terms with him, which is impossible if they take him to court'. The behaviour of any given man will vary in degree of responsibility from time to time as his circumstances change; the paternal role is very ill defined. 'In flagrant contrast to the idealized picture of the little woman and the patriarch' says Katrin Fitzherbert, 'you get the jarring reality of a tough bossy woman ruling a family with an ineffectual man or no man at all. Underlying all this runs a strong current of hostility between the sexes with the woman frequently giving as good as she gets.' In recompense for the heavy responsibility she must assume for her children when they are young, often being father as well as mother to them, as she grows older she expects them to look after her. All the children are especially close to their mother. The only institutionalized method of husband-catching is to go and live in concubinage with the man of your choice. Any girl who played the waiting game would find herself almost past childbearing before her man could afford to keep her and any offspring.

These are the patterns of sex relationships that West Indians bring to England with them, and they explain a good deal of what to us seems anarchic in their sex mores. Settled West Indian communities here are beginning to frown on irregular affairs and mothers tell their daughters to keep away from men, unfortunately without explaining to them why, or giving any useful sex instruction. The girls begin having intercourse at the average age of seventeen, according to Katrin Fitzherbert. Often the girl is initiated by an older man who exploits her because she is less demanding than older women. When she becomes pregnant, sometimes while still at school, and she gets to know about the English Child Care system she is eager to have her baby taken into care so that she can go on with her own training as typist or nurse, or just go out to work. Here she has greater earning power than she would have had where she came from and this makes her a more desirable partner for either common-law or legal marriage, so in England she is more likely to find a steady mate. Both partners work hard to buy a car and house of their own. Although concubinage and illegitimacy rates are high by our standards, marriage is steadily on the increase among them. From Mr Ayre

I learn that, under pressure from various English officials, some West Indian girls are marrying before they have given serious thought to the question of a suitable life partner, with the result that soon they are clamouring for divorce, as their expectations of married life have been unsuitably high. Basically they do not conceive of any relationship between having children and marrying. One might put it that it takes them a long time to grow up sufficiently to be ready for a stable marriage. Meanwhile, they have their children. In their country of origin under the extended family system, this way of doing things worked well enough. But here, living isolated in one room with her little ones, the single West Indian girl who wants to go out to work (and most of them do) must either find a childminder or lock them in while she is out. Neither practice is satisfactory. Many childminders take in a number of infants in comfortless conditions, without adequate supervision. Children locked in at home are frequently left without toys, and spend much of their time asleep. There have been many instances of children knocking over the burning paraffin heater in their room and being severely injured. In these cases of apparent child-neglect, the Children's Office may be tempted to take the children into care and some mothers are delighted with the idea. This is carried so far that according to Katrin Fitzherbert, once a girl has had one of her children put into care she expects her subsequent children also to go into care, even when she is in regular association with a man or married. The Service is there and she feels she has a right to use it, for her own ends, and without thought for the well-being of the children. To get her own way over this she will make terrible scenes, shouting and cursing, and will tell endless lies as to the non-existence of relatives, neighbours or friends who could look after the children while she is at work. Mrs Forbes of the West Bromwich Children's Office mentioned to me a six year old girl in care whose mother wanted her back to take the new baby out in the pram while she herself got on with the housework. In the long run most West Indian women will doubtless adjust themselves to English customs and delay having children until they are married – if they can manage the contraception problem. Perhaps the answer is the fitting of the intra-uterine contraceptive device? But those who are still in our schools need a great deal of help in sex education from under-standing teachers – far more than we are currently giving our white pupils. According to Mr Ayre, some of their sexual superstitions are amazing: for instance, that the number of children one ought to have corresponds to the number of the ridges showing on one's navel, and that if one doesn't have the full quota the blood will mount to one's head and cause insanity.

We are now in a position to see the English-born West Indian children in our schools in relation to their home backgrounds. They enter our reception classes at the age of five, in many ways backward as compared with white children, because their parents have literally no idea of their psychological needs, have left them untalked to and unstimulated, without toys or play materials to exercise their finger muscles and their sense of precision or stimulate their imaginations. They do not know how to tell the time, to distinguish left from right or colours one from another, they cannot count. Their vocabulary is as poor as that of any deprived English child and often they are quite unused to being taken out by their mothers. Coming from homes where people wash themselves in a basin filled from a jug, they are unaccus-tomed to taps and plugged basins. The flushing W.C. also is new to them; they have only had the use of a bucket. They have to learn how to drink school milk through a straw, how to hold pencils, crayons and scissors. What I have myself seen in reception classes of infants schools bears out the information supplied by Mrs Forbes, Mr Ayre and Katrin Fitzherbert. Most five year old West Indian children need intensive social training before they can begin where white five year olds begin. They are therefore among the strong candidates for nursery schooling. To them even play space is a luxury; hence their frenzied pushing and rushing in corridor and playground, during which children often get knocked down. For although untrained at home, they are healthy, strong and very boisterous.

Teachers of all age groups complain of the loudness of their voices. This may be explained by West Indian habits in their country of origin, where the outdoor life prevails and people shout to one another across the fields or in crowded streets. They find it unnatural to lower their voices. So even when the children are asked to talk quietly, their classroom conversation soon resumes its clamorous character, which may be supplemented by drummings of the fingers or pencil on any hard surface. The teacher finds he must constantly exert himself to prevent the noise from becoming a din in which concentration for most would be out of the question. It is not that they want to be difficult but that they cannot grasp why anyone should want less noise.

It is often commented by teachers that many of the West Indian children are 'dense' or slow at school work. For this there are several explanations. Some West Indians do not appreciate shades of meaning in English as spoken here, an inability they will not readily admit to. But those in whose homes there is little talk of any kind and what there is is in a Creole dialect, cannot be expected to keep up in class with English children who have picked up at least some glimmering of how English should sound from television. Many also think that only physical activity counts as work and are unwilling to apply themselves mentally. From these and perhaps other causes they are in general intellectually slower than their white classmates and those Asiatics who have mastered the language difficulty. So there arises among them that peculiar combination of slow wittedness with the bounce of their high vitality which teachers find hard to cope with. And when thwarted they are said to become sullen or aggressive and will shout the teacher down if he lets them. Their parents resort to spanking to hold them in check and will advise the teacher to do the same. If he does not believe in corporal punishment (and the Plowden committee recommend its abolition in primary schools), he is now in a spot. The child expects to be disciplined with blows; he will not take seriously anyone who does not smack him when he has been naughty and will proceed to go to lengths undreamed of by white children. For instance, a little girl in one junior school used to annoy her teachers by displaying herself in her underpants to the class. When an H.M.I. visited the school, she ran through her repertoire of attention-claiming tricks for his benefit and when he spoke to her reprovingly she retaliated by calling him 'Bloody bugger!' It is not easy to restrain such children, nor can they be removed from the school simply for being tiresome. Perhaps those people who want slappings outlawed will explain how they propose to deal with this sort of behaviour, which seems to cry out for the shock treatment of a sharp smack. Are we to treat West Indian children in our schools differently from white ones? How can we prevent them from disturbing the normal running of an entire class? The really difficult cases do not respond to the permissive methods current in English education.

But the most difficult West Indian children are undoubtedly those born abroad whose mothers have left them there with their grandmothers until there was enough money to pay their fares to England. Such children, according to T. Burgin and Patricia Edson are often spoiled and babyish when they arrive here.[1] They are immediately subjected to multiple shock due to change of surroundings, our incredibly damp and chilly climate, and finding the half-forgotten mother probably living with a strange man and younger children whom she has had since she left the Caribbean. Under these conditions, to enter an English school, in which an unfamiliar brand of English is being spoken and an unfamiliar type of ethos is taken for granted, cannot be a re-assuring experience. To a child who is not very clever it must be so discouraging that he feels quite unable to co-operate. This is where the worst behaviour difficulties begin. At one secondary modern school for girls in the inner ring of Birmingham I was told that almost all the girls who had recently come to join their mothers presented behaviour problems. There were girls who played truant in order to go shoplifting in the city centre and then telephoned the Head to tell tales on one another. Every portable object in the school has had to be kept locked away if it is not to vanish. Even so, a padlock was broken off a cupboard door and cups and saucers and the teapot inside, belonging to the Women's Institute, were smashed. The perpetrators of this prank were not identified. The worst case was a girl found to be sleeping on a mattress in a derelict house near the school, it was thought with a man. She was quite out of parental control. Whenever she came to school she was dressed in very tight fitting clothes, and from the playground she signalled to men passing by. After a prolonged struggle the Head, unable to persuade her to change her ways, expelled her, and reported the case. She next turned up in a

[1] T. Burgin and Patricia Edson, *Spring Grove*.

Remand Home where she drove the warden almost frantic by stripping off and displaying herself in a lighted window overlooking the street. When I asked whether white girls in the school imitated these antics, I was told that so far as was known they did not. It was other coloured girls who copied them. In a mixed secondary modern school with over 30 per cent of coloured children, I was told that it was disconcerting to find that coloured children who had been given positions of responsibility with the intention of encouraging them were abusing these positions by bullying other children into giving them sweets, comics or pocket money in return for 'protection'.

In all the schools I have visited where there are 30 per cent or more of coloured children, the staff complained of the persistent flow of petty thefts, brawling and other misdemeanours among the coloureds; to get at the truth about these incidents they found almost impossible, because the coloured children appear to have no feeling whatever for accuracy of statement. They tell lie after lie without any inner tension such as would betray itself by involuntary clenching of the hands. Relaxed and happy, they say whatever at the moment seems to them convenient and a few minutes afterwards will be stoutly maintaining something quite inconsistent with it. Repeat the two statements back to them and they are not in the least abashed! To find out what actually took place by the cross checking of the various versions from more than one child is a strenuous mental exercise and very time-consuming. In the face of conflicting evidence a white child will usually break down and confess, but West Indian children more often raise their voices to reiterate the latest story. 'Only someone of great conviction and personal magnetism can hope to succeed with them, preferably a man, even in primary school', I was told.

With even settled West Indian children of secondary modern age, it is still true that 'one telling is never enough for them'. They have to be reminded day in day out to wear a tie, to bring with them a pen and a pencil. One teacher discovered that the only way to avoid wasting the time of the class on these trivialities was to make them all report to him every morning wearing ties and displaying pens and pencils. Few of them have any idea of time. It follows that appointments are seldom kept and the expedient of

7

dropping a note to their parents to remind *them* of the appointment can be equally useless.

In schools of mixed sex the disciplinary problem becomes acute. For you can deal out physical punishment to boys in a boys' school, and by using shock tactics from the outset in a girls' school you can make girls break down and cry after which they usually improve their ways. But in a mixed school, men teachers do not like having to speak sharply to girls and the boys have to be sent out of class to the Head or Deputy to be chastised. We are confronted with the fact that modern permissive methods are unsuitable to West Indian children. As their numbers grow, especially in the lower streams of schools, the disciplinary problem will have to be faced and some realistic policy evolved, having regard both to their own long term well-being and that of the other children in the class. Katrin Fitzherbert asserts of West Indians that they are highly adaptable and when placed in care have been most successfully anglicized. So it appears to be up to teachers to stand firm and apply pressure whenever it is needed. There probably should be consultation between teachers who are faced with these classroom problems, perhaps in the form of conferences of which notes could be circulated or published. Lest it be thought that West Indian peculiarities are all on the debit side, schools with 30 per cent or more of coloured children often find their cricket, netball and general athletics teams almost entirely made up of them, and there are highly praised West Indian prefects.

Asiatic children have completely different family and cultural backgrounds, easier for us to grasp but likely to prove more difficult to modify in the long run than those of the West Indians.[1] The Indian tradition is more liberal and flexible than the Pakistani, for although Indian boys and girls remain part of the extended family system whose head may still be in India, their girls, when they leave school here, are allowed to work in hospitals, for instance, or in shirt factories. The chief problem among them is linguistic and is hardest to solve with those who have come to join their families here when they themselves are already of secondary-school age. This problem applies to all Asiatics. To come to a

[1] For information on the cultural and home backgrounds of Asiatic children in England I am indebted to Mr T. G. Ayre.

strange country with an unfamiliar climate, and often be compelled
to live in conditions far poorer than they were used to at home (for
of course they share the accommodation troubles of the West
Indians) is hard enough; inability to speak the language is a factor
in the situation which makes all the others more painful, preventing them from asking for help or advice, and putting the women
and children of the family at the mercy of their landlord and of the
father of the household, who together act as interpreters and go-
betweens. It is hardly surprising that Asiatics cling together,
forming small colonies in blocks of old property with their own
shops nearby, where people of their race sell their own foodstuffs
and clothing materials. They really do not want to be separated.

The Pakistanis, being Muslim, are very conservative in nature,
and whatever they profess, have small inclination to abandon any
features of their own culture in order to become 'assimilated' here.
Two things dominate their lives: the Mohammedan religion, and
the extended families to which they belong. Their religion dictates
what they shall wear, what they may eat and how it must be prepared, although neither the clothing of the women nor the diet is
really suitable to our climate. The girls wear a pyjama costume of
thin satins or brocades, far too flimsy for English weather during
most of the year. Those of them who have not adopted woollen
underwear can still be seen shivering under their cardigans and
coats. The purpose of the pyjamas is to hide the legs, so that men
will not 'have bad thoughts' when looking at them. Indeed, some
of the East Pakistani girls, a very old-fashioned group from small
jungly villages in Bengal (of whom there are many in Birmingham) still refuse to take off their pyjamas in school for lessons in
physical education. Few Pakistani males seem to have overcoats
or macintoshes; instead they wear layer upon layer of sweaters
under their jackets, but when all this has been soaked by rain it
takes several hours to dry out. Muslim cooking is in the kosher
tradition, which means that part of the school dinner may be
inedible by Pakistani children, nor is their own food always
appropriate for our climate. Parents often will not allow girls to
be taught English methods of cooking in school and this is reasonable enough since kosher meat cooked by English methods is
tough. Again the English ways of making garments are useless to

girls who may always dress in the standard Pakistani manner, and so they often say that their parents will not let them learn English-style sewing; they are to stick to their own traditional embroidery. If they make English friends who invite them to their houses, the English must be prepared to cater in the Muslim manner, for no concession may be made in the food laws laid down by the Prophet. Up to the present, the way of life enjoined by their religion, and the extended family group in which that way of life is perpetuated, have combined to bar anything beyond the most superficial conformity to western manners and attitudes. Many of the mothers are still virtually in purdah, mingling only with their own families and with women; their inability to speak English has had the effect of keeping them in this position. Local authorities put on afternoon classes in English for them, and some progress is now being made in helping them to find their way in our towns. On some Birmingham bus routes it is usual to encounter little groups of them on a shopping expedition to the city centre, boarding the bus like a flight of gaily-coloured birds, all chattering in their own tongue. Jangling their bracelets and hoisting their large-eyed children on to the seats, they make the white Brummie feel as though he had strayed on to a trip overseas. They do not even look at the rest of us; for them we seem not to exist.

Those of their children who were born here and have learned some English are docile and polite in school, and some of them are highly intelligent. Opposition to school policy tends to take the form of saying 'Yes, oh yes!' but continuing as before. What teachers do complain of is the unusual proclivity of the boys to get into fights with knives, and that Oriental deviousness which is bringing about the introduction of graft into school life – after all bribery is a normal part of their parents' way of life. In the playground, too, they can be just as noisy as West Indians. Among Asiatics, however, it is the language difficulty which causes most trouble in school. Among those newly arrived in England it is extreme. They cannot understand what the teacher says, cannot follow a lesson, cannot be given instructions except through the mediation of classmates who speak their own dialect, and so cannot safely be allowed into laboratories or workrooms with dangerous apparatus which must be carefully handled. Nor can their parents be communicated with at any level but the crude one permitted by an elementary grasp of English. Misunderstandings inevitably arise on both sides. Until prolonged English instruction has been given, little else can be taught. The unhappy child, bewildered and on the defensive, is suffering from a strong dose of cultural shock, complicated by climatic shock. This accentuates his normal tendency to cling to the family group, and not try to mix with children of other races. In Birmingham a team of peripatetic teachers of English as a second language goes round the schools, giving instruction by the direct method to classes of non-English-speakers, who must then make what they can of the other classes with the help of classmates who speak their own tongue. It is not highly satisfactory, but until proper reception centres are opened to give intensive courses in English and the English way of life, what else can be done? I watched one such class at work, about a dozen Asiatic girls who were using a sort of reading laboratory. Since they were already literate in their own languages, the concept of the relationship between printed or written symbols and spoken language was already familiar and they seemed to be making headway. Nevertheless some Asiatics who come here at the age of 12 or more, are still not literate in their own tongue. The need for reception *centres* is obvious in view of the number of boys and girls aged up to sixteen who will still be arriving to join their families here until about 1973. West Bromwich, Walsall and Wolverhampton have reception classes for non-English-speakers instead. In *Spring Grove*, Burgin and Edson describe the development in an inner ring school in Huddersfield of a Special English Department to which all Huddersfield's non-English-speaking children are directed. It has developed from a single seminar into seven graded full time classes in English as a second language, also using the direct method. Some children become proficient in English much more rapidly than others. When they are ready, those of primary age usually go into a class at Spring Grove Primary School (housed in the same building as the Special English Department) with an age group a year younger than themselves; when they have shown that they can cope with the change, they are moved up into their own age group. Similarly children of secondary age spend a term in the top junior class of

Spring Grove before leaving for the secondary school nearest their own home. So successful has this arrangement proved that none have had to be returned to the Special English Department. A difficulty for that Department however has been the arrival of newcomers in ones and twos throughout the teaching year, who cannot be integrated into existing classes. It is suggested that these be kept together in a 'waiting' class with an Urdu-speaking teacher who can introduce them to English ways until at the beginning of a term they can form a class or join existing classes.

Some people suppose that language is not necessarily a barrier at the *beginning* of a child's education. The Spring Grove staff decided to test this assumption. For an experimental period in 1961 they put six non-English-speaking immigrant children aged five directly into the ordinary infants' reception class. 'Success was very limited, in spite of the attempts of the teacher to give individual attention where possible. . . . They were handicapped, not only by their inability to understand English but also by their lack of pre-school training in such things as number-recognition, counting, building games and constructive play. Consequently their progress in both conversational English and in their class-work was very slow compared with that of the other children in the class, although after the initial setbacks, they eventually showed some slow but quite definite signs of advancement. With one, two or three immigrant infants placed in an English class, success would be likely, but with higher numbers the teacher cannot give the necessary extra attention'.[1]

An interesting complication is that some older Indian children arrive here able to read English fluently aloud without understanding much of what they read or being able to converse in English; they have been trained to 'bark at print'.

At one secondary modern school for girls I was invited to chat with Asiatic girls in their teens but soon found that their traditional evasive courtesy made it impossible to find out from them how they reacted to English life, English weather or the living accommodation. Television appeared to play an important part in their lives, suggesting that they learn much about our own culture from our programmes; teachers told me that they would watch 'the

[1] T. Burgin and Patricia Edson, *Spring Grove*, p. 37.

most wretched programmes with absorption'. They must find in them much to draw back from! It will not be surprising if their religion and their fathers combine to keep them averted from the more permissive elements in our way of life. For the typical Pakistani family is dominated by its head male. His word is law. Many a girl who has been through our primary and secondary schools and been encouraged by her teachers to look forward to a clerical or other job, finds that within a week of leaving school she is married off to the husband selected for her by her father and within a year she has her first baby. One such girl who had stayed on at school until she was sixteen and was considered very intelligent managed to go back to visit the Head two years later: she already had two children and her only way of getting books to read was by arranging for her sister who was still in school to borrow them for her from the school library. Every week her family went to the public washing baths next door to the public library, but her husband would not wait for her to go into the library and change a book. No doubt this situation will be gradually modified since such girls will be able to teach their own children English in the home, and as it dawns on their menfolk that women's earnings will be useful to the family the custom of segregating them may slowly break down. But customs closely connected with religious observances are unlikely to change very fast. The one that teachers would most like to see become obsolete is the observance of the fast of Ramadan for a month in January and February when no Muslim may break his fast between sunrise and sundown; children of late-rising parents may go twenty-four hours without food or drink and have been known to faint in class. Naturally their work falls off very noticeably. With the change in our own Daylight Saving Programme at least children will be less likely to come to school in the morning unfed. We must also bear in mind their segregationist reactions to English disapproval and hostility as expressed in the press and in common behaviour. Unless we can make these people feel that they *could* if they wished make themselves at home here, they are going to remain indefinitely bunched defiantly together.

Now what are the general effects of this wave of coloured immigration on our schools? There is agreement between Heads

I have spoken with that the thieving and lying, the wanton destruction and sexual irregularities in their schools have increased alarmingly side by side with the influx of the coloured children over the past three and a half years, incidents traceable to coloured children being out of all proportion to their numbers. (Figures supporting this contention cannot be quoted, being highly confidential.) It may be that only a few of the coloureds are responsible for the bad behaviour, but if so, these few are creating a grave disturbance. As few as three such children can upset the work of a class of thirty. Their teachers become steadily wearier with the unremitting effort of holding them in check, sorting out from the tissue of evasions and lies what they have actually been up to, and keeping the class quiet enough for work to go on. But apart from these difficult cases coloured children, as soon as they number more than six or seven to a class, have a way of making their presence felt by their raising of the level of noise, and, if West Indian, by their boisterousness and intractability. Inevitably a class containing as many as 30 per cent of coloured children will work more slowly than a class with none or only a few. English educational methods are quite alien to Asiatic tradition, and English discipline is too permissive for West Indians. It is chiefly in inner ring schools that the higher percentages of coloured children are to be found, up to 80 per cent in a few London and Birmingham schools and ranging from 30–60 per cent in others. Their presence in such numbers accentuates the already formidable difficulty of keeping staff in our slummier areas. It is hard enough to work with entirely white classes of underprivileged youngsters amid those grim surroundings in out-of-date buildings: introduce a sizeable proportion of coloured, some of them difficult, and the situation proves too much for many teachers. In this way the serious problem of high teacher turnover, unsettling children who need prolonged contact with familiar teaching staff, becomes even worse. It is now proposed that special allowances be paid to staff in schools in the bad areas. In addition, many such teachers will require extra training relevant to the satisfactory teaching of coloured children. They will need to understand the cultural and home backgrounds in this country of the various ethnic groups, their styles of classroom behaviour and ways of dealing with it.

Training colleges should draw on the experience of teachers already used to a high proportion of coloured in their classes, and with their help and that of such people as welfare officers, put on special courses for the growing number of teachers in urban areas who are confronted with the difficulties I have been describing. Probably no trainee teacher should leave college without having attended such a course, since given the high mobility of teachers themselves it cannot be guaranteed that any urban teacher is never going to need the information. A text-book on the subject begins to be required, and perhaps it should be put together by a symposium of teachers experienced in this field with social workers and social anthropologists.

In primary schools it has often been noticed that children of all races mix unselfconsciously. But this is not necessarily a prelude to integration. For as adolescence approaches the racial groups in secondary schools begin to draw apart. This may be partly due to the onset of courting, when like seeks like, and partly to warnings from parents to have less to do with 'the others'. It may also be in part a crystallizing of racial groups around their own late-comers, who need help in their unfamiliarity with our language and customs.

The Department of Education and Science last year adopted the policy of dispersal of coloured immigrant children throughout the schools of each local authority so that there should be no more than 30 per cent of them in any one school. But if teachers who are used to them are justified in claiming that six or seven are as many as a class can absorb without a falling-off in educational and social standards, and given the continuation of present trends in coloured birthrates, how many of the schools in a city such as Birmingham will be adversely affected by dispersal in the foreseeable future? How will the ratios in any given school be kept steady without continuous dispersal, involving much travel for both white and coloured children, although it is not considered good for children to be frequently uprooted? And finally, so long as streaming continues, even if only to the extent of separating out the 'fliers' and the very dull, how would it be possible to avoid a heavy concentration of coloured children in the lower streams of schools, a segregation by both ability and colour? There is no easy solution to these problems.[1] To disperse coloured schoolchildren effectively means dispersing their families throughout the area controlled by the local authority, and there can be no doubt that the electors in the areas where there are pockets of coloured population would be strongly opposed to the deliberate spreading of the coloureds over the area as a whole. Another point against dispersal is that Muslim parents say they intend to keep their daughters away from mixed-sex schools to which they are directed. (This is also a difficulty for comprehensive reorganization of schools through the grouping together of boys' and girls' schools.)

So far nobody seems to have seriously considered asking coloured parents what their own preferences are. It seems probable that few Muslim communities would wish to be broken up in order that dispersal of the coloured children throughout schools could be facilitated by dispersal of their families. It is not so easy to guess what West Indian parents would like. They came to this country expecting to be treated as ordinary members of the community, living freely among the white population and not in any way discriminated against. Despite frequent official protestations that no discrimination is intended, there can be little doubt that it takes place, and many West Indians in this country feel sore as the evidence mounts up. I have already referred to local authorities who dodge housing coloured applicants on municipal estates, putting them instead into old sub-standard property. For some years now the sale of a house in a white street to coloured people has usually been accompanied by local indignation, and followed by a tendency of the whole street to go coloured, producing a growing pocket of people who feel themselves cold-shouldered by the rest of the neighbourhood. On this basis it is not easy for integration to get going. Repeated slights may have made the coloured newcomers sore and suspicious before they get the chance to settle down on a friendly footing with those whites who do not want to move away. One is reminded of Jewish families who used to long for assimilation into non-Jewish communities, wanting only to be accepted and taken for granted as

[1] Since the above was written there are signs that genuine racial integration is proceeding apace in the newly opened comprehensive mixed school at Mount Pleasant, in Balsall Heath, Birmingham. The lower age groups are unstreamed.

indistinguishable from their neighbours. Nearly always there was someone maliciously waiting to nose them out and start the whispering about 'the Yids'. Without the goodwill of the whites, coloured families cannot even get as far as did the Jews, for their complexions proclaim their otherness.

Even if they find a house to their liking among whites who are friendly with them, the coloured immigrants soon find that there are firms and individuals who refuse to appoint them to jobs. School heads have told me that it is always harder for a coloured school leaver to find suitable work than it is for a white one of similar ability. It is not always the employers who are to blame, for some workers will not work alongside coloured people. One Birmingham firm which tried to apply a fifty-fifty ratio of white and coloured among its work-girls found that as this proportion was approached, prospective white employees on looking round the shop decided against accepting work there and in the end, apart from a few old hands who did not want to leave, the entire staff was coloured. It is as yet too early to say to what extent coloured entry to the professions is limited. But there certainly exist in this country numbers of coloured people who in their countries of origin were qualified teachers, journalists, or secretarial workers, but who cannot find work over here of the sort for which they were trained. It is of course possible that their qualifications are not quite right by English standards, but their disappointment can be understood. They have joined the ranks of their countrymen working on public transport, and in hospitals and factories, but naturally they hope that their children who have been educated in our schools will fare better. The schools do their best by these children and it is heartbreaking for teachers to hear of the promising youngsters turned down for job after job, simply because of the colour of their skins. For when a white and a coloured leaver from the same school are sent to be interviewed for a given opening how often does it happen that it is the coloured one who is chosen? Surely the white cannot always be the more suitable applicant? What can be done in schools to prepare coloured youngsters to face such mortification without bitterness? Must the answer be, 'Nothing'? There are firms which accept coloured apprentices for engineering courses; we need a similar elimination of colour prejudice from the minds of *all* those whose task it is to select people for jobs. For this type of discrimination is the one which leaves the worst scars and is best guaranteed to produce resentment in the coloureds against the whites, a resentment already gathering force in a multiplicity of splinter movements against racial discrimination. We can expect this resentment to seep backwards into school life, still further complicating the difficulties of teaching coloured children. Coloured school leavers of all races are affected but the most actively resentful are the West Indians who have always regarded themselves as British and expect fair treatment. In these circumstances it may not be so easy for them to decide whether or on what terms they still want integration with the white population and dispersal, whether of families throughout an area, or of children throughout schools.

Yet whatever children and their parents think today, there is an answer to all these questions, a public policy which must be put into practice if we are to avoid a repetition here of the civil disturbances, the deaths and injuries and destruction of the summer of 1967 in Detroit, Newark, Milwaukee and other places scattered over the U.S.A. We must not let coloured people congregate in any sort of ghetto, we must not discriminate against them either educationally, in housing, or in selection for jobs. Justice has to be done and be seen to be done. And this will involve the enormous educational effort, in school and elsewhere, of getting English people to understand the members of the various coloured groups and accept them as individuals of differing worth just as we are ourselves, to be worked beside and lived next door to. This means that it is not only teachers who will need to have courses on the culture and psychology of the different immigrant groups. The children in our schools should themselves be discussing and being instructed in these topics as they approach school leaving age, for few of them are going to spend their entire lives isolated from coloured people. The sort of crude colour prejudice I encountered among quite intelligent Borstal boys, with whom I had a discussion group in 1963, will have to be eliminated by an increase of knowledge. We have in our schools to bring up a generation of young people prepared to be fair to one another irrespective of skin colour. The newcomers on their side have to be shown what is expected of them in England and to meet the white natives half-way. This last point is worth making because lots of English towndwellers by now have had experiences of being elbowed aside in queues by coloured immigrants and of meeting the assumption on their part that they will be allowed to overcompensate for their disadvantages.

So far relatively few coloured youngsters have entered our grammar schools. As time passes more of them should be doing so. From what I have heard and seen in classrooms it appears to me that when they can speak English fluently some of the Asiatics will make hardworking pupils, many of them with mathematical ability; surely we have here a source of ability of a type already insufficient in this country to meet the growing demand. We need coloured technicians and instructors; at the same time we must take care to train white youngsters to accept the coloured mathematics teacher as a respected specialist. As a first step to this situation we must ensure that educational selection on a non-examination basis never works in such a way as to keep coloured children of ability out of the higher streams. A difficulty with West Indian children is that since so many of them are uninterested in learning, they are likely to form a hard core of the under-privileged in a society in which trained intelligence gets a good many of the rewards. This is a good reason for keeping some form of fair and above-board selection for entry to higher education, if not the eleven plus. It must be seen and accepted by all as fair that all those able to profit from training to 'O' level and beyond are so trained irrespective of race or background. If some coloured people do not qualify for the better jobs it must be seen that this is because they are duffers or lazy and not because they are not white. Here we have again in a more extreme form the problem already raised by working class English children of poor home background who fail to get grammar stream places in proportion to their initial tested ability, the children whose performance falls off as they pass the age of eight.[1] The typical West Indian home has many of the disadvantages noted in the homes of some working class white children – lack of books, of conversation requiring the skilled use of English, and of the assumption that education is

[1] cf. J. W. B. Douglas, *Home and School*.

important. If the answer to the problem of the English working class child is partly to enrich his educational experience in school, and partly to prevent him from being segregated in some group without good future prospects, how much more are the same solutions appropriate to the duller of the coloured children. It is increasingly clear that we cannot allow ghetto type schools to proliferate and that we must set about dispersing coloured children from those already in existence. And this must involve us in dispersal of coloured families throughout the towns where they congregate and even over the country at large, and a corresponding education of the public to accept this situation.

Nor will all the adjustments of attitude need to be made by the whites alone. Coloured children and their families need to digest the fact that their arrival here in such numbers is seriously complicating the working of our overtaxed social services and parts of our educational system, and that nobody can assume that the necessary changes in attitude, the special training of teachers, the nursing of tolerance and understanding among white schoolchildren, their families, and employers and workpeople at large will be accomplished in a short time. It is a situation in which everyone concerned has to be patient and to make his contribution.

The problem type of coloured child cannot be allowed to hinder the work of a whole class, but he usually has white classmates who are almost as tiresome as himself. Do we spread these characters, *whatever* their colour, over all the classes of a school, or do we concentrate them in groups which admittedly will need special handling? On the utilitarian principle I must agree that the least amount of mischief might well result from their concentration in small groups, like fever patients. The experiences of teachers with late arrivals from abroad in secondary schools suggests that a lower age bar should have been imposed, say ten, which would have enabled all such to receive intensive training at a reception centre before going to secondary school and would have curtailed some of the long family separations that have done so much damage. It may be also that we shall have to regress for a time, however regretfully, in matters of discipline. It is not clear how many schools with 80 per cent of coloured children in their reception classes were visited by Lady Plowden's committee members; one must say that free discipline is not suitable for schools with coloured children who are troublesome in their own particular ways. What is involved is a slowing down of the revolution in disciplinary methods, and to refuse to see any need for this is unrealistic.

I have argued for the dispersal of coloured families throughout our towns and of coloured children throughout our schools, accompanied by special courses for teachers who will deal with them, and a deliberate thorough-going educational policy of fostering mutual understanding and tolerance between white and coloured people. This is not merely the fairest policy, but the only one that can prevent us from running into incalculable social troubles in the future. Finally I cannot stress too strongly that the coloured people themselves are under some obligation to reciprocate tolerance and generosity (when they meet these) with stout efforts to fit in here with a minimum of fuss and to learn that neither bumptiousness, evasiveness nor graft is generally acceptable in England, permissive though we may be. Nothing irritates an English person more than the suspicion that immigrants, whatever their race, are out to exploit him. We do not want to see parts of our country (which is none too roomy) being taken over by exotics with alien traditions and high birthrates unless we can be convinced that they genuinely wish to join the existing community and make a fair contribution to its prosperity. This is the American line, 'You can come in but you must *join*'. The Americans have not applied this a hundred per cent to their coloured citizens but it is what we shall have to do.

VIII · Educational Selection: Comprehensives and Streaming

We now approach the much discussed question of what form the organization of our schools should take. This question can only be rationally answered with the purposes of education in mind.

The prevailing view *used* to be, especially in grammar school circles of the 1920s when I was a girl, that the chief purpose of education was instruction, whether as an end in itself or by way of training for a job. The function of schools was held to be the inculcation of examination-passing skills, and any other aim was treated as merely incidental. So, good pupils were those who learned the greatest number of those facts and judgements, arguments and techniques, which can be displayed in the examination room. A teacher was primarily an academic expert in chemistry, Latin or whatever, and his excellence lay in his ability to transmit what he knew to his pupils. He presented the academic ideals of accuracy and the desire for knowledge. Each child was to be induced to work hard to acquire knowledge and skills. He was praised and rewarded when he succeeded, and occasionally, when he was merely seen to be doing his best, blamed and punished when he did not try, and discredited when he made a mess of it. Regular comparison with his classmates kept him up to scratch by means of marks for written work, examinations, and his place in the form order. The competition was supposed to be as fair as possible, with each pupil earning his marks by his own efforts, but in fact nobody could prevent parents from helping with homework, nor pupils from helping one another. For instance, I have known girls spend half the evening telephoning around about an awkward translation exercise or an algebra problem which would not come out. But, theoretically at least, all pupils were locked in rivalry.

This competitive aspect of the educational system has actually been very much intensified and extended since my own childhood.

For in the 1920s competition was restricted to selective school entry and university scholarship examinations, together with the internal examinations of the selective schools – and there were at that time relatively few such schools. Most children expected to go to the local authority's elementary schools and to leave at fourteen, so that they took no part in the educational rat race. Success or failure in life for them depended on other things than a good school record. But since the war an altogether more systematic effort has been made to provide a good education for every child with the ability to profit by it. Children are being sorted out into groups according to their scholastic achievements and then given different sorts of education in accordance with their presumed ability. Far more today take 'O' and 'A' level G.C.E. examinations than used to sit for their earlier counterparts, and far more now enter the universities. An attempt is being made, even if it is not an altogether successful one, to enable those with the best brains, regardless of social origin, to qualify for the jobs which require most intelligence. The educational system has thus assumed the function, originally suggested for it by Plato, of sorting the population into an intellectually superior class, destined for positions of responsibility, and an inferior class suitable for life's less exacting roles. To a far greater extent than ever before, academic success is now a stepping-stone to power and influence, whether as administrator, persuader or researcher. This trend becomes more pronounced as knowledge expands and professional skills multiply. Employers increasingly demand a fistful of 'O' levels, even for the most straightforward white-collar jobs. Many believe that the most effective approach to this programme of selection-by-scholastic-ability is still that of my own old grammar school, with its strong emphasis on academic instruction and unremitting rivalry. Now that educational qualifications are openly valued as job credentials giving access to particular levels of income, rather than as signs of achievement, it follows that children of seven may already be engaged in competition for better standards of living to come.[1] The general organization of

---

[1] For pressure of parents on their children to pass the eleven-plus examination as a first step towards the better paid jobs and middle class status see D. N. Swift, 'Who Passes the Eleven-plus?' in *New Society*, vol. III (5th March, 1964).

English education at present is still adapted to this approach, and so we have segregation of children into grammar, technical, secondary modern and 'special' schools according to their supposed abilities; uniform examinations set and marked outside the schools; streaming within individual schools; many teacher training courses more concerned with the study of school subjects than with that of children and their social environments; and the general classroom layout at secondary school level placing the instructor in splendid isolation and the pupils in their rows of desks in front of him. All these features fit the general pattern of competitive endeavour to acquire a specified body of information and skills.

Yet while the economic pressures in favour of this educational pattern have been, if anything, on the increase, the general trend among teachers and educational theorists has been in quite another direction. The current movement is against segregation of children by ability, and in favour of teaching together those of all grades of ability in unstreamed classes, and in comprehensive schools. It is against competitiveness in the classroom, favouring instead co-operative projects. It is against strict discipline, and in favour of a relaxed classroom atmosphere in which children are free to move around and talk as they go about their enterprises. The policy is to attract or coax them into learning instead of driving them. It is against the use of external examinations for grading at entry to the secondary school. It is against fixed syllabuses and in favour of merging topics that used to belong to different subjects. It is against concentration on academic subjects and in favour of introducing into school syllabuses such activities as car-maintenance, bee-keeping and creative writing. It is against putting very much stress on accuracy in spelling or grammar, and in favour of emphasizing imagination and spontaneity as scholastic virtues. It is against the style of teaching in which the instructor authoritatively tells the pupils what they are to believe or do, and in favour of a style in which pupils find out for themselves the answers to their questions. If the old attitude implied that education was a sort of Grand National, with children trying to race one another over a series of obstacles, the new attitude presents it as somewhat more like Lewis Carroll's Caucus Race, in which the runners start and finish at whatever point they fancy, and everybody gets a prize. Finally, the new attitude places on teachers the responsibility, not merely of instructing their pupils academically, but also of developing their aesthetic and moral sensibilities, improving their characters, and fitting them for responsible citizenship of their society. The avowed purposes of education have been multiplied.

The new movement cannot be said to be the outcome of educational research. Nobody so far has been able to prove, and perhaps nobody will ever be able to prove, that unstreamed education is academically more effective than streamed education.[1] Nobody has proved that relaxed discipline produces better scholastic results than strict discipline, nor that project methods leave a bigger deposit either of information, or of enthusiasm for learning, than text-book methods. And equally, nobody is able to prove the opposite of these assertions. The factors involved in the educational process are so many, and vary so much from one situation to another, that proof may turn out to be unattainable. The biggest obstacle to making valid comparisons between the results of different teaching methods is that one can never know how much to allow for differences in the skill and personal attitudes of the teachers themselves, which might be the most important factor of all.[2] Education, like so many other human activities, is a field in which we often have to rely on the plausible hunch. The new movement may be seen as the educational aspect of a general trend towards more relaxed and permissive living which my husband and I examined in *The Permissive Morality*, a trend which has affected the upbringing of children, the treatment of criminals, sexual standards, social welfare policies, and even habits of dress and speech as well as what is done in schools.[3] If this is so, it is unlikely that the trend in education will easily be arrested or reversed. What we have to do is to assess its effects wherever assessment is possible, and make sure that we have a clear view of the arguments for and against its various manifestations, bearing

[1] For full discussion see p. 131 *et seq.*
[2] This point is brought out in the summary of results in the N.F.E.R.'s preliminary report on Streaming, *Plowden Report*, Vol. II, App. 11, p. 589.
[3] C. H. and W. M. Whiteley, *The Permissive Morality*.

in mind the new functions thrust upon schools by present-day social pressures. Should we be accelerating or checking the new movement?

I propose to consider in some detail the pros and cons of the selective principle in education. Our established system of selective secondary schools, and of streaming within most schools, is based on certain assumptions. It is assumed that, since children vary very widely in the quality and the diversity of their scholastic abilities, it is not desirable that they should all be given the same type of education. On this view 'equality of educational opportunity' cannot mean all children getting exactly the same training; instead it will mean every child getting the sort of training which is thought to be best suited to his capacity. So there should be either a variety of schools, or comprehensive schools with a variety of courses, catering for the needs of the many types of children. It is further assumed that differences of ability are to a considerable extent innate and permanent, and that by appropriate tests it is possible to sort out the cleverer from the duller and assign each child to his proper group to receive a suitable kind of tuition. Corresponding to differences in talent, there are different roles in society to which different grades of ability are appropriate. It would be disastrous if people attained positions of responsibility when they had neither the wit nor the training for exercising it. These tasks requiring high intelligence are usually among the most highly paid, for high intelligence is a commodity in short supply (although a striking anomaly of the situation is the extraordinarily high rate of pay for entertainers). Thus in sorting out the cleverest children we are also sorting out those destined for the better-paid jobs.

Another important assumption is that teaching is more effective when the children in the class are all at about the same grade of ability. If a teacher tries to give the same instruction and the same tasks to very clever and very dim children together, and matches his instruction to the needs of the clever, the dull will be bewildered and probably disheartened and humiliated by their failure and will begin to hate their lessons. If on the other hand, the teacher tries to go at the pace of the duller children, the cleverer ones will become bored while they wait for a lesson to be repeated that they mastered weeks ago, or for a point to be explained which they grasped at the beginning of the lesson. So they will not be acquiring as much knowledge and skill as they might, and, what is more important, they will not be getting into the habit of using their minds at full stretch. Being under-occupied and bored, they will become discontented and scornful of classroom activities. Such bright children without enough to occupy their restless minds can become the most dangerous type of delinquent, because the most ingenious, for they believe that they are in a world which is not made to their measure. And if the teacher addresses himself to the average children, who make up the bulk of the class, those at both extremes are going to feel neglected. Anyone who has to teach children of mixed abilities together, if he tries to treat them as a homogeneous group, is bound to fail with some part of his class. It is therefore desirable that classes should consist as far as possible of children whose abilities are not widely dissimilar.[1]

Finally it is assumed that competition is a useful stimulus to learning; more work it is thought can be got out of children if they are set the goal of passing an examination, reaching a higher place in class, obtaining promotion from one stream to another, or just beating the boy next door. And the incentive is all the stronger if it can be truly claimed that the children who get through their examinations will go on to become the bosses of those who do not.

In pursuance of these principles, the established system has evolved two kinds of selection. Firstly there is selection into four different types of school, grammar, technical, secondary modern and those for the physically or mentally handicapped; secondly there is streaming – selection within the school of the brightest children from each age group to form a top stream to be taught together, of the next brightest to form a second stream and so on in as many gradations as there are teachers available for the age group. Segregation by school happens for the most part only after the age of eleven, but segregation by stream can begin quite early in the primary school. The British educational system is

---

[1] Even parents share this view, believing that slow children receive more attention when placed together, and that bright children working together are not held back by slower ones. Cf. *Plowden Report*, Vol. II, p. 587.

peculiar in the thoroughness with which it applies these principles of segregation. To sort out the children of a school into streams, there has to be a constant series of tests conducted within it, first to make an initial assignment and then to find out which children have been incorrectly assigned and should be transferred. To sort them out into the different types of secondary school the main instrument has been, and to a considerable extent still is, the massive eleven-plus examination, the uniform test taken by all children of a given area. Later on, there will be a further selection process by means of Ordinary and Advanced levels of the General Certificate of Education, to apportion the abler youngsters between the superior and inferior universities, technical colleges, colleges of education and other institutions of advanced education.

The reforming movement attacks the whole system of selection in principle. The final stage of selection, for university level, is not as yet under serious attack. There have been criticisms of the way universities make their selections but only with the intention of making such selection more efficient. It has not as yet been suggested that universities should abandon their habit of admitting only the best qualified students in favour of the American system of admitting anybody who reaches a not-very-exacting standard. (The American system involves turning out large numbers of the incompetent after a year's trial, a procedure expensive of the time and energy of both staff and students. The argument that an extra hundred people at the back of the lecture theatre makes no difference to the lecturer is invalid, since those hundred must have their written work marked, must be accommodated with seminar sessions, examined, housed and provided with all student facilities). But all the other elements in the selective system have come under attack. It is argued that the tripartite structure of grammar, technical and secondary modern schools should be replaced by comprehensive schools admitting all kinds of children and giving a full range of instruction. And it is argued that within individual schools streaming should be replaced by the teaching of unstreamed groups each containing a wide range of ability.

The case against educational segregation can be put under five headings. In the first place, it is argued, educational apartheid, like racial apartheid, is a system of unfair discrimination in favour of one group at the expense of another. Grammar schools receive far more money per pupil than secondary moderns. They get the ablest teachers because those who teach in them receive on the whole higher salaries, easier conditions and more respect. Grammar schools can therefore pick and choose their staffs while secondary moderns take what they can get. Grammar schools have many more teachers for a given number of pupils so that instruction is both easier for the teacher and more effective for the pupils. They are provided with more books, more laboratory equipment, more assorted teaching aids, more space, better sports equipment, pleasanter and more commodious buildings. Similar advantages are enjoyed by the A streams in streamed schools. Many teachers prefer to teach bright children rather than dull ones. (There are some who are moved to specialize in very backward and handicapped children, the sort who get into 'special schools' and remedial classes, but hardly anybody wants to grapple regularly with an ordinary bottom stream.) So the best teachers tend to get the A streams; if they are forced to take D streams they may go to other schools where they can be sure of taking A streams. Besides, it is the A streams in a school which produce its success records in any public examinations that are taken, so a Head who wants his school to enjoy a good academic reputation will naturally concentrate his most effective teachers on this prestige-earning group.[1] The lower streams are commonly assigned to those teachers who have no choice – people who are not good enough to find other posts, beginners, temporaries, or unfortunates who are out of favour with the headmaster. Among them are many of the least efficient teachers, who as a group are also the most likely to become fed up and leave if they can. Thus it happens that the lower streams get less of that continuity of teaching which they actually need more urgently than cleverer children do. A class may have several changes of teacher within a year, being faced each time with a new personality, another approach, perhaps even a modified syllabus. For instance it is not impossible for one class to cover the same period in history over and over again, or to have unfortunate gaps. And the duller children are less able to rise to

---

[1] cf. J. Partridge, *Middle School*, for a telling statement of C and D stream conditions in a secondary modern school.

the challenge of such happenings. Separation of the dull from the bright always means less and worse for the dull. In the same way the lowest stream will always be last in the queue for the use of any extra equipment, since in any case they take less care of it and make less obviously valuable use of it than upper streams. Being the hardest to teach, they will be the likeliest to be set to work on odd jobs instead of studying. And so on. Because the expenditure of effort and resources on clever children seems so much more rewarding, this kind of discrimination is inevitable as long as segregation exists. It must result in a steady widening of the gap between the groups. 'From him that hath not shall be taken away even that which he hath.'[1] The advantage that the bright child had in the beginning is steadily increased year by year by the more efficient training he gets. He gains proportionately more, whereas the duller child, who might have made something of his talents if taught with maximum skill, makes nothing of them under the care of inexperienced, incompetent, temporary or disgruntled teachers.[2] Again, a class of clever children is on the whole an interested and comparatively keen class; any child in it who wants to work can get ahead in an encouraging atmosphere. But when you assemble in one room all the least able children in an age group, some because they are naturally stupid, and some because, for reasons of temperament or personal history, they are opposed to learning what they are asked to learn, you will produce an atmosphere of overall hostility to teacher and lessons, in which the efforts even of any good teacher who happens to come in will become concentrated on keeping order, and any child who might have made an effort to learn will be thwarted by the attitude of his classmates. These discriminations against the duller child are inseparable from the system: they can only be got rid of by getting rid of the principle of segregation.

Secondly, it is argued, the constant procedure of testing and classifying, while it may cheer and stimulate the successful, disheartens the rejected. And the 11-plus failures inevitably outnumber by far the successes – by three to one over the country as a whole. But the proportion of failures can be far higher than

[1] St Matthew, ch. 25, v. 29.
[2] cf. J. W. B. Douglas, *Home and School*, p. 96, footnote.

this, as for instance in the city of Partridge's *Middle School*, where it varies between ten and just under seven failures to each success. So the principle of segregation is labelling the great majority of our children inferior. From this point in childhood they are already marked out for the less rewarding and less respected places in society. Although they themselves may not particularly notice or mind about this (plenty of them would sooner stay at the local school with their friends than be transferred to a grammar school among strangers at a distance from home), those of their parents who are anxious and ambitious will not let them forget it, and will end by transmitting some of their own disappointment. Unfortunately every year the anxious and ambitious parents form a bigger proportion of the whole.

Streaming has the same effect as 11-plus selection, but if anything it is intensified. For the child in the bottom stream receives daily reminders that his *is* the bottom stream. We may expect that the effect of having it rubbed into him that he is not clever will often be that he loses interest in studying, and decides that it is not his cup of tea. The educational system having rejected him, he in turn rejects the educational system, and devotes his energies to learning as little and causing as much trouble as he can. It is true that Musgrove has reported that grammar school children show consistently stronger traces of dissatisfaction with school than secondary modern children.[1] But bearing in mind that it is not the grammar school children who smash the windows and break up the furniture in schools, one wonders whether his research techniques have done anything more than record the stress symptoms of pupils irritated by academic competition but nevertheless essentially accepting it, whereas the secondary modern children are not at all worried about academic competition because they have given up taking it seriously, and have little use for school. Once a child is put into a lower stream and labelled 'slow', he is far less likely to learn well than if he had been given a more encouraging rating. It is plain that the attitude of a teacher to his pupil makes some difference to the way he approaches that pupil, the extent to which he presses him to do his best, the patience and perseverance he is prepared to use with him, even the way he looks

[1] F. Musgrove, *The Family, Education and Society*.

at him. Few teachers approach a D stream with pleasure or warmth of interest. Very few give it as much encouragement and sympathy, as much care and trouble as they would give to a higher stream. It is for this reason that the assessments made of a child's ability at the beginning of his school career tend to be self-confirming. Once he has been classified as superior, all the circumstances conspire to make him actually superior. Once he has been classified inferior all the circumstances conspire to slow down his progress.[1] The classification itself may be in part cause of the very difference on which it is supposed to be based.[2]

This self-confirming tendency of the selection system would not matter so very much if the original selection had been fair and accurate. But another objection to segregation is that the original selection is not fair and accurate enough to justify the sharply different treatment accorded to the different groups of children. Of children admitted to grammar schools on the basis of the eleven plus examination, 20 per cent according to the Crowther Report do not pass G.C.E. O-level in any subject, and 38 per cent gain only one or two passes. In his study of the Woodlands Comprehensive School in Coventry, Thompson found 'no significant correlation at all between the eleven-plus rank order and either of the two sets of school examination results' (during their first year).[3] How can segregation claim to be either fair or effective until there is a more reliable method of picking out those children who have the capacity to learn well from those who have not? If the original selection is either arbitrary or faulty, we shall simply be picking out some children who are not necessarily the ablest for a better education than others, which seems indefensible. Now there is

[1] J. W. B. Douglas in *Home and School* reports that in streamed samples from junior schools those in the upper streams improved their test scores between the ages of 8 and 11, whereas those in lower streams deteriorated. In the lower streams, the brighter children showed a greater average deterioration in the test scores than the duller children. By contrast, the less able children in the upper streams were stimulated by good teaching or by competition. Douglas's sample consisted of all the children born in one week of March 1946.

[2] See D. Thompson, 'Towards an Unstreamed Comprehensive School' in *Forum*, Summer 1965. In this study evidence is produced that children of secondary school age do better when they are in a class labelled 'A' and so believed to consist of the brightest pupils, even when the members of this class have in fact been assigned to it at random.

[3] Ibid.

plenty of reason for arguing that there is a great deal of arbitrariness and inaccuracy in the ways that children are actually sorted into 'better' and 'worse' groups. For instance, children move up in batches of complete age groups, each batch including those born in the autumn along with the others born in the following summer. But the autumn born have had one or two extra terms in school at a time when this advantage was vital, that is to say, they have had the opportunity of learning more. So when streaming begins a larger number of them get into the upper streams and once there get the better teaching, are pressed to work harder, respond to the livelier atmosphere, and in due course do better in their eleven-plus – not because they had any more ability than others of their age group but because they were born at a different time of year.[1]

This is not the only fortuitous and irrelevant factor that influences the streaming of children. Their initial placing is partly determined by teachers' impressions.[2] Yet there is good reason to believe that teachers' impressions of a child's intelligence are influenced by things other than intelligence; by his tidiness and cleanliness, by his manners (the open friendly child who talks readily makes a better impression than the timid or the surly child, and a far better impression than the rude and hostile one), by the degree of his eagerness to adopt the good pupil role, and even by their knowledge of the family, district or social class he comes from. But even when the judgements of teachers are strictly based on objectively measured performance, it is not possible to take present performance as a reliable indication of future potential. For one thing, different children develop at different rates. One who is backward at eight may be forward at thirteen or vice versa. Given equal opportunities children move up and down a great deal in their relative abilities and places in class. Again, a child's poor performances in a given year may be due to illness or

---

[1] See H. Clarke, 'The Effect of a Candidate's Age', *British Journal of Educational Psychology*, Vol. XXVI, part 3, pp. 207 ff. Also, *Plowden Report*, Section 347, Vol. 1.

[2] Brian Jackson in *Streaming* tells how he found that in his sample of 660 primary schools the most popular bases for allocation to streams were the class teacher's judgement and the infants school report, with externally devised tests in reading, arithmetic and spelling at the bottom of the list.

emotional disturbance at that time; but once he has been graded on the basis of this unrepresentative performance he may find it very hard to change his grading. And there are other more long term factors that may cause his school performance to fall well below his intellectual potential. Among children of equal natural ability, those will do better who have homes in which there are books to read, intelligent conversation, and a variety of toys and play materials[1]. Those will do better who have fewer brothers and sisters, probably because they get more of the adult attention and conversation.[2] Those will do conspicuously better whose parents are interested in education and keen that they should succeed, and such children are less likely to suffer permanently from an initial setback because their parents will go to the school and pester the teachers to find out whether they can be moved up. The opposite case, of the C-stream child 'trapped in the net of minimum expectation' whose parents do not realize that he has 'never seriously been in the race', and do not wish him to suffer from anxiety or other effects of the pressure to excel, is aptly described by Brian Jackson in his chapter on Honey Bell Infants' School in *Streaming*. All the advantages I have mentioned have a marked class bias in their distribution for it is in the working classes that we most frequently find the homes without reading matter, without genuine conversation (talk being mostly restricted to orders, complaints, imprecations and stereotyped comment in a minimum vocabulary), without space for doing homework, without constructive toys, and with many brothers and sisters competing for space and amenities. Similarly it is working class children who tend to hamper their own progress in school by uncouth manners, lack of social *savoir-faire* (by the middle class standards that many teachers have), or hostility and suspicion towards school and teachers, and it is they whose parents are most likely to be too uninterested in their progress to make contact with the staff. So the principal bias in the selective system is one against the intelligent working class child. Studies such as those of Douglas and

[1] Brian Jackson in *Streaming* points out that at seven, future A-stream children have comics their parents approve of, jigsaw puzzles, expensive constructional sets, word games and playing card games calling for the development of new logical skills.

[2] J. W. B. Douglas, *Home and School*, pp. 83 ff.

of Jackson and Marsden[1] have shown that these children do not succeed educationally in proportion to their innate capacity. The selective system aimed at picking out the brighter children is failing to pick out a high enough proportion of the cleverer working class children, and is unduly favouring middle class children who are less well endowed. (Yet however unfair it may seem, this class bias in the selective system is not entirely unreasonable. Children from homes unfavourable to education are more likely than the others to fall behind with their work, break down, or give up. So long as selection continues, there is the same sort of reason for a certain bias towards middle class children in streaming or selecting as there is for a bias in favour of men as against women for professional training; it is not the women's fault that they are liable to pregnancies and childbirth, but all the same they are less likely than men to give value for training. Similarly, working class children are less likely to give a good return for educational expenditure, although it is not their fault that their families are unco-operative or even inimical to education. There is a certain ambivalence on this issue detectable in the work of such writers as Jackson and Marsden who, while strongly protesting that so few children get the opportunity to rise out of the working classes up the educational ladder, describe with evident distaste those in their sample who have managed to do so, and have ended by becoming middle class in their outlook.) We can try to counteract the influence of the unhelpful home. We can keep rooms open in school in which homework can be done quietly under supervision. We can provide the books to read. If the home is very bad, we can even take the child into care or find him a subsidized place at a boarding school. But unless we are going to get rid altogether of family life, it will continue to be one of the determining factors in educational success.

If selection for streaming within schools is exposed to all manner of bias, the eleven-plus examination shows up by comparison as objective and fair! Indeed, nothing can be less biased than the uniform public examination. But it has corresponding defects. It is a single once-for-all test. The child who happens to have a feverish cold or a stomach ache, a bereavement or an emotionally

[1] B. Jackson and D. Marsden, *Education and the Working Class*.

disturbing quarrel to spoil its performance on the critical occasion
has missed its chance for good. A formal examination puts a heavy
premium on the possession of good examination nerves, a useful
quality no doubt, but surely not sufficiently important for one's
entire future to depend on it. Besides these individual hazards there
are the collective ones arising from variations in teaching quality
in different schools and classes. Even at the highest level I have
known an experienced G.C.E. examiner say 'I find I am not
assessing candidates so much as schools'. A child's performance in
an examination depends on the efficiency of the teaching he has
received as well as on his own ability. It is notorious that some
schools have a good reputation for external examination successes.
Children who get through because they have been well taught, or
worse, because they have been efficiently crammed, enter grammar
schools at the expense of abler children who have not had this
advantage. Of course the really brilliant are unlikely to fail: the
dull are certain to. But among the many who stand somewhere
between the brilliant and the mediocre it is largely a matter of
accident as to which are chosen and which rejected. Those who
just fail to get into the grammar school would probably do as well
there as those who just succeed in getting in. Pattinson[1] as Head
of a newly established mixed technical-grammar school found
when he looked at the eleven-plus marks of the first year's intake
that as few as fifteen marks made a difference of a hundred places
in the complete eleven-plus list. We cannot guarantee that all
those selected are actually of better quality than the best of the
rejected. For instance, Thompson[2] in the Woodlands Comprehensive School, Coventry, found that of the sixty-two boys (about a
quarter of the year's intake) who under a selective scheme would
have earned grammar school places by their eleven-plus performances, half were surpassed in their first year's school examinations by others who would *not* have been admitted to grammar
schools.

Since selection is so unreliable, it may seem reasonable to try
to remedy its mistakes by making plenty of provision for 'second

[1] W. Pattinson, 'Streaming in Schools', *Educational Research*, June 1963
[2] O. Thompson, 'Towards an Unstreamed Comprehensive School', *Forum*,
Summer 1965.

chances', moving up and down children who have been wrongly classified, and keeping the grading constantly under review. In fact, provisions exist, but the overall amount of redistribution seems to be quite small (in streamed schools it is usually smaller than teachers and parents believe it to be). Certainly it never reaches the proportions needed to correct all or even most of the errors in the original selection. And wherever there is a big difference between the work of one stream and that of another, or between the work of different schools, there are good reasons why there should not be many transfers between them. The promoted child will always lack some of the grounding that his new class mates have had, and in subjects like mathematics and languages this could be critical for his progress. At the same time, he does not know the teacher, the other children, or the customs of his new class and has all this to learn as well as what he has missed academically. The demoted child will find life academically easier, but socially just as hard as the promoted child, and will carry the additional burden of disheartenment. A number of children in a class who are feeling lost, whether because they have been promoted or demoted, will hinder teaching efficiency and class cohesion. All these difficulties are much aggravated in school-to-school transfer so that it seems that the value of the expedient is limited.

A fourth objection to the selective system is made not on educational but on social or political grounds. The criterion here is harmony and understanding between social classes in the community. The objection is to the general system of meritocracy, whether in Plato's version or that of Michael Young.[1] If you mark off the members of your community into a number of clearly distinguished groups, if you so arrange things that members of any one group will meet, talk, work and play only with other members of that group so that for them the members of other groups are merely people passed in the street, or hearsay acquaintances, then the habits and standards of the different groups will diverge more than in a freely mixing community. They will read different books, play different games, speak different dialects. Consequently when they do encounter one another they will have

[1] Michael Young, *Rise of the Meritocracy*.

difficulty in finding much in common. Communication will be imperfect, friendly contact almost impossible. The superior group who have to give the orders will not be properly understood by the inferiors who have to obey them (unless trouble is taken to use only those verbal expressions with which they are familiar), and the efficient working of the society is bound to be impaired. Along with imperfect mutual understanding will go imperfect sympathy. They will be unable to see one another's point of view and will tend to regard one another as not really human. This hostility and misunderstanding between social classes has long been a standing obstacle to general prosperity and happiness in England. With democratic forms, equality of opportunity, and universal education, we had hoped to get rid of it and inaugurate a society where people of all ranks would be able to work together. But educational segregation hinders this aim. Even those who do not care about the ideal of the brotherhood of man must care about the hindrance to efficiency in a complicated industrial society which comes about when managers and men are filled with mutual mistrust. Industrial friction is constantly blamed not on malpractice nor on irreconcilable differences of interest, but on the failure of communication (the inability of management or government to explain to workers what is being done and why it is necessary). This difficulty is likely to continue as long as the leaders and the led belong to different sections of society, live different sorts of lives, never mix, and are unable and unwilling to talk to one another and be understood . . . because having so little contact with each other they think of each other as ludicrous stereotypes of Colonel Blimp and Andy Capp. In the past the gulfs in society were perpetuated by the system of inheritance. Now they are produced anew by differing levels of education. This educational principle of class division may indeed be fairer than the hereditary principle, but is in its way more dangerous. For while the country squire would have a different upbringing from his gamekeeper, he might very well have much the same character and interests. But the educational system of today segregates people who are likely from the outset to have different temperaments and inclinations, and goes on to intensify the existing differences.

There is one more objection to the selective system. The process of selection itself has an enormous effect on the character of all the teaching given and the general spirit in which it is conducted. Since the future of each child depends so much on his examination results, and since entry to grammar schools and universities is necessarily competitive (for it depends not only on reaching a given standard but on outdoing enough of the other candidates to get one of the places available) the whole tone and atmosphere of most schools has to become competitive. Children must be encouraged to work hard so that they will win the race and gratify their parents and teachers (who care about these things far more than most of the children). They have to be taught to treat each other as rivals, so that if one helps another out this is cheating because everyone ought to succeed on his own merits. And this need to assess each child independently runs counter to the need to train children in the art of co-operation. Some people prefer the idea of a society full of competing individuals, where everyone is striving to outdo the Joneses and general progress somehow emerges from individual self-interest, but others prefer the idea of a society in which people are as ready to help their fellows as themselves. Surely on this fundamental issue of the whole spirit of our social life we should not be committed merely by the need to pick educational winners! We ought not to allow the technical requirements of educational selection to impress on our children the vision of life as a rat race. We ought to make the utmost positive use of the tendency of children to form groups and gangs to which they feel loyalty and find a place in our educational arrangements for fostering these tendencies so that they will help the educative process. Instead, we are doing our best to ensure that most of the groups formed voluntarily by children are hostile to school, teacher and society.

The effect of the rat race ethos comes out plainly in those university students who have most completely assimilated it, and prospered as a consequence. The type of student who will never read a book, attend a lecture, write an essay or even talk about anything concerned with his subject of study unless he can be assured that there is likely to be a question on it in his final examination, is all too common. The more we insist on learning a school subject as a means of moving up the competitive ladder,

9

the harder we make it for ourselves as teachers to put over the view that the subject is worth studying for its own sake. The Ph.D., as it normally is in Arts subjects, stands as a depressing witness to the competitive view of education, for a vast number of the theses are not aimed at the satisfaction of any lively interest on the part of the student, nor at the discovery of any piece of knowledge that will be useful or interesting to others – for few theses are ever read by anyone except the examiners. They are mere tests of competence and endurance, like the tasks imposed on Psyche by her jealous mother-in-law as a condition of admission into the heavenly circle.

If the system forces the children into competition with each other, it does the same for the schools. From the point of view of the ambitious parent, the main function of the primary school is to get his child into a grammar or at least a technical school, so that he will be assured of a good place in society. What he learns in the process is seen as of secondary importance. And the main function of the grammar school will be to get him into a university. So the reputation of a school will depend to a tremendous extent on the number of children it gets through the competitive examinations. Every year *The Times* lists in order those schools which have got most university places, and those colleges which have got most first-class degrees, with the implication that these are the best schools and the best colleges. In a steadily successful grammar-type school, departmental heads will compete to get the highest number of university scholarships among their pupils, and to persuade the cleverest pupils to choose their particular subjects, so that if the head of the classics department is a stronger personality than the head of the physics department, it often happens that more of the clever pupils opt for classics than for physics. The main priority is given to top scoring. We have already noticed the tendency for the most competent teachers and the best teaching conditions to be pre-empted for the brighter pupils. This tendency is strengthened when there is a scholarship class from which the Head expects the successes which will raise his school's reputation. Partridge observes how, even in a secondary modern school not officially committed to preparing for external examinations, all the teaching arrangements were geared to the effort to get about a dozen boys through a second chance attempt at the eleven-plus examination. The remainder of the school suffered for the sake of these few examination successes. And of course *Middle School* is not alone in this practice.

But the best way to get children through examinations is not generally the best way to educate them for their future lives. If a teacher aims at examination successes, he is going to concentrate his energies on what will tell on examination papers, and skimp everything else. He will go over set books time after time until the pupil knows them perfectly and hates them intensely. Even as he crams, he will blinker his pupils against other interests. Many teachers do not like doing this sort of thing, and resist the pressure on them to do it, but all the time the pressure is there, and those who yield to it have an advantage over those who resist. Moreover the examination-minded teacher will persistently try to filch time and resources from his colleagues in other subjects, regardless of the balance of the children's education. Brilliant children don't need to be taught like this, and do not thrive on it, but *they* are going to get their 'A's' at Advanced level anyway. It is among the great mass of moderately endowed borderline children that cramming can make the difference between success and failure. Too often in the process of achieving the desired result the child loses his spontaneity, his liking for and interest in the work, his sense of the point and purpose of his studies and their relation to the rest of his life. The examination determines the class syllabus too, but some of the things that it is important for a child to hear about are not easily tested in a written examination, and these are likely to be omitted. It is always so much easier to test factual knowledge than the capacity for making inferences. We can indeed test the ability to spot an inferential pattern when this is presented in the terms of an intelligence test, but what we cannot test is the ability to scan the *total* environment for the presence of such patterns (of which there may be none present that are relevant to us) and this scanning is what we must learn to do in our everyday lives. Similarly, aesthetic appreciation is not readily testable. Yet both of these are essential to a way of life which draws on a high proportion of the individual's latent creativity.

Everyone of these criticisms deserves respect. Taken together, they constitute a formidable case against the practice of streaming as it is done in many schools today, and against tripartite segregation. Accordingly humane and progressive teachers are beginning to experiment with unstreaming schools which hitherto have been streamed, and the Department of Education and Science is officially committed to complete comprehensivization of its schools. But there are many people who seem not to realize that the substitution of comprehensive schools for the tripartite system does not necessarily put an end to selection. The majority of the comprehensive schools so far established are still streamed. In place of grammar schools and technical schools and secondary modern schools we find something like grammar, technical and modern streams within the comprehensives. To those who believe in streaming there is indeed a stronger case for selective streaming in a comprehensive school than in either a grammar school or a secondary modern with their narrower ranges of abilities. If the brightest pupils in the comprehensives are to be prepared for Advanced G.C.E., they must inevitably work at a different level from their schoolmates, during a great part of their secondary school lives. One cannot suddenly acquire the habits of working more accurately or at greater depth: these have to be cultivated from an early age in aspirants to university education. 'The fear that pupils over the whole range of ability will be taught together in academic subjects is quite unjustified by the facts in all but a tiny minority of comprehensive schools', say the compilers of the 1966 Report on London Comprehensive Schools.[1] What a comprehensive school *can* nevertheless do is to delay the streaming of its pupils until a higher age than eleven, to the advantage of late developers. Or it can practise setting as an alternative which avoids some of the pitfalls of streaming. Under setting the pupils in a given age group are divided for certain subjects into ability groups, each recruited from all the forms at that level. It is most often practised for mathematics and English, but sometimes for languages too. Its advantage lies in enabling pupils to work together, in every subject for which there is setting, with those whose working pace most nearly approximates to their own. Those in the

---

[1] I.L.E.A., *London Comprehensive Schools*, 1966.

most advanced set for mathematics will not necessarily be found in the corresponding set for English or foreign languages, for it often happens that those who are quick at mathematics are slower at languages. Some schools have the same setting for mathematics as for science, and the same setting for English as for foreign languages. For subjects other than those setted, children remain in their own form unit. So there is mixed ability work in most subjects and a child who is slow at one of the setted subjects may show a compensatory brightness in one or more of the others, work at his own pace in all of them, and not feel an all round failure. Setting is a device enabling aspirants to higher education to prepare themselves intensively for it, without at the same time relegating anyone to the deadly experience of a totally D-stream life. Advocates of unstreaming without even setting up to sixth form level will have some difficulty in demonstrating how this is to be done by aberage teachers without impairing the academic standards of would-be university entrants. So far they have not convinced many Heads of comprehensive schools. Some form of selection is operated in almost all of them, whether it takes the form of streaming, setting, or the steering of unacademic youngsters away from the more academic options at whatever age this takes place. Since getting rid of the eleven-plus examination by making our schools comprehensive does not eliminate selection we need to be careful that the methods of selection used inside the schools are not less fair and efficient than the eleven-plus.

The comprehensive school has one great and indisputable advantage over the tripartite system. Because of its size, it can offer a wide range of alternative courses to suit different abilities and tastes, so that in so far as children do specialize while still in school, they can specialize in subjects they are keen on and are good at. The comprehensive school need not have a uniform programme for all. Specialization and selection, often by the device of 'options', can begin at any age that is found suitable. Pupils can be moved from one stream, set or option to another far more easily than they could be moved from one school to another. Each child has therefore a better chance of receiving an education that suits his capacities.

To reap this advantage a comprehensive has to be really large (there has been much argument as to *how* big, but certainly much bigger than existing segregated schools). This raises a serious problem of accommodation. Even if we could afford to replace all existing school buildings with purpose-built new comprehensive schools, there would not be enough sites available of the proper size in crowded urban areas. So local education authorities are trying to carry out their instructions to 'comprehensivize' by the method of grouping together a number of schools in different buildings, often long distances apart, and calling such a group one school. Children at entry are housed in one set of buildings, then at a later stage moved to another set and so on. *The Times* of September 18th 1967 contains two letters complaining of the difficulties of this kind of arrangement. In one letter, the secretary of the Ystalyfera Grammar School Parents' Association in the Swansea area of Glamorgan points out that the local education authority is proposing to establish a school of 1,620 pupils housed in six separate buildings, 'a small cramped grammar school, a disused primary school, a tiny college of further education, a secondary modern school (all in a built up hilly area with no room for expansion or for recreational facilities), a pre-war secondary modern school over six miles away from the main site and another 3.3 miles from the main site'. And in another letter the head of the mathematics department of Tredegar Comprehensive school, Monmouthshire says that as a result of the combination of four schools into a comprehensive with 1,200 pupils, 'I teach 15 A-level pupils in a room measuring 20 feet by 12 feet by 7 feet; I have been forced to teach in the staff room with other members of staff present; to spend morning break standing because 26 male staff have to use a room containing 12 chairs; to commute to another block 2 miles away in the middle of a session; to watch someone teach on the gymnasium balcony while physical education goes on below.' These instances give some idea of the general inconvenience of such improvised comprehensive schools – and the Tredegar school is the pilot scheme for its county. Another difficulty in this sort of arrangement is that when children are moved from one building to another as they pass from one age group to another, they have to familiarize themselves with a new environment, which the duller children always seem to find trying.

The younger ones miss the leadership and example of their seniors, and the problems of organization, already formidable in a large school, are aggravated.

Size also appears to make discipline more difficult. 'Size makes it more difficult to achieve and maintain a high standard of discipline . . . individual staff, sometimes far from the centre of authority, escape the censure that a smaller, more tightly knit staff might impose . . . I have noticed (in two different schools) a tendency for staff to abandon the task of corridor supervision and to retire to their own class rooms where control is easier.'[1]

Another drawback for any comprehensive school in a socially homogeneous area, such as we find in modern housing estates and commuter suburbs, is that a school which takes all the children from a given neighbourhood will necessarily reflect the character of that neighbourhood. The depressed and deprived areas will supply batches of unpromising children unable to support effective grammar streams or sets. Instead of the more and the less academic types of schools, as at present, we shall have more academic and less academic comprehensives. Of course backward schools already exist in backward areas, but at present a clever child can get out of such a school into a grammar school; under the comprehensive system he will never be able to get out. Even given the new additional equipment and special allowances for teachers in schools in problem areas, the brighter children in these districts will inevitably find their opportunities curtailed. Ambitious parents will still try to get their children into the schools serving the better neighbourhoods and will thus have an additional motive for moving into the better neighbourhood themselves. There is here a clash between the principle that a school should include a wide range of social classes and types, and the principle that it ought to be the neighbourhood school taking all the children of the district without discrimination, integrated with its surrounding community and serving as a social centre for it. In a socially homogeneous district the school cannot fulfil both ideals. To overcome this difficulty, the Inner London Education Authority are requiring the heads of their comprehensive schools to fill their schools

[1] Incorporated Association of Assistant Masters in Secondary Schools, *Teaching in Comprehensive Schools*, p. 128.

with a representative cross section of ability, even when this involves refusing local children and admitting outsiders. The Inner London Education Authorities' Report on their comprehensive schools unfortunately does not tell us for how long this practice has been going on, and whether the outsiders imported to correct the balance of ability in a school are becoming socially integrated into its life.

A major reason for advocating comprehensivization has been the hope that it would lead to plenty of mixing among children of different origin and different levels of ability and would thus act as a check to the division of society into non-communicating groups. But we cannot be sure that such mixing will take place except temporarily and to a limited extent. In one comprehensive school in the Midlands, boys of the grammar, technical and modern streams respectively refused to play together in any one football team, and each stream had to have its own team. If mixing does take place there is reason to doubt whether it will make very much difference in the long run. It seems likely that youngsters from different social groups integrated in a single school will mix freely enough until they approach puberty when pairing-off begins, but pairing usually takes place only between boys and girls from the same or adjacent social groups.[1] Similarly it is often noticed in English schools that the different racial groups begin to sort themselves out about the time of puberty. The clash of cultures, whether of race or social class, first shows itself unmistakably as soon as boys and girls begin to choose a 'steady', and with good reason. There are few people who would enjoy spending a lifetime tied to somebody whose basic values are utterly different from their own. The problem of communication and prejudice between social classes is a serious one. I am not convinced that comprehensivization by itself will be able to contribute very much towards solving it. The *quality* of the education given, especially to working class children, is likely to be more relevant. The better people are educated, especially in the humanities, the better they are placed to understand one another.

These reflections are borne out by the findings of T. W. G.

[1] Compare A. B. Hollingshead, *Elmtown's Youth*.

Miller in his study of *Values in the Comprehensive School*.[1] He found no evidence for the hypothesis 'that the comprehensive secondary school contributes to the development of social unity within the community'. What he did succeed in finding was evidence of a smaller divergence both in scholastic and leisure interests between boys in grammar and modern streams in comprehensive schools than that between their counterparts in segregated schools.[2]

Segregation in the forms of streaming, setting or guided options is to be found in most comprehensive schools. But if we seriously want to eliminate all the social and psychological ill effects of educational segregation, we shall have to resort to unstreaming our schools. Headmasters who have done this often speak or write enthusiastically about the improvements in morale which ensue. William Pattinson, describing his own experiences of unstreaming the non-selective secondary school of which he had been Head, says, 'Educationists want conditions in which every pupil can attain his optimum standards, and this is only possible if he is socially at ease, a happy contented member of his group or groups . . . Those who have unstreamed a streamed school report first and emphasize most the changed and improved atmosphere in it. Head teachers refer to the vastly improved emotional stability of all pupils, but especially the less able, to improved group relationships, and to better behaviour and a decrease in aggressiveness and delinquency. They report not only a happier school with fewer problems of discipline, but more satisfied parents, keener teachers and a better classroom atmosphere. Some in addition claim improved eleven-plus results after only a short period of non-streaming.'[3] E. Harvey, after two years as headmaster of a junior school with 320 children in the West Riding, unstreamed it on an age basis with a range of six months in each class (somewhat reducing the spread of achievement due to a twelve-month age range). He says, 'After four years without streaming I have a happy and enthusiastic staff, all of whom prefer the present organization, the standard of work has improved and relations with parents are

[1] T. W. G. Miller, *Values in the Comprehensive School*, pp. 89–90.
[2] Ibid, p. 66.
[1] W. Pattinson, 'Streaming in Schools', *Educational Research*, June 1963, p. 232.

excellent.'[1] D. Thompson, reporting on the Woodlands School, Coventry, says in his summary of conclusions, 'There is evidence that streaming produces or at least perpetuates undesirable social attitudes, and that relaxation of streaming produces a better attitude towards school on the part of many children who in a streamed situation would have been badly behaved.'[2] The verdict of the Inner London Education Authorities' inspectors on their experience of unstreamed schools was, 'The unstreamed class can be a satisfactory social unit, there being no obvious tensions arising from disparate ability.'[3] Other writers in the pages of *Forum* have testified to improved morale and general behaviour following unstreaming, presumably because it does away with the frustrating influence of the bottom-stream environment.

The misgivings felt concerning both comprehensivization and unstreaming are mainly due to fears that abler children will not be made to realize their full potential. As regards comprehensives, what information there is at present is inadequate either to dispel or to confirm this fear. R. Pedley, argues that whereas in segregated schools 'some 11 per cent of each age group proceed to take a good G.C.E. around the age of sixteen' ('good' meaning five passes), schools in the Isle of Man and Anglesey, the only completely comprehensive areas in Britain, scored $16\frac{1}{2}$ per cent and 14 per cent respectively in the years 1959-61, and twenty comprehensive schools in various other parts of the country averaged around 14 per cent, although several of them were heavily creamed by grammar schools.[4] This looks encouraging. But crude comparisons of this sort are very liable to error. 'Attempts to compare examination results of grammar and comprehensive schools . . . are bound to mislead unless account is taken of the spread of ability of the pupils concerned; and this has never been done on any proper statistical basis.'[5] It is clear that a large number of children in comprehensive schools are winning examination successes which they would not have won if they had gone to those

---

[1] E. Harvey, 'Unstreaming a Junior School', *Forum*, Spring 1960.
[2] D. Thompson, 'Towards an Unstreamed Comprehensive School', *Forum*, Summer 1965.
[3] I.L.E.A., *Inner London Comprehensive Schools*, 1966, p. 62.
[4] R. Pedley, *The Comprehensive School*, pp. 96 ff.
[5] I.L.E.A., *Inner London Comprehensive Schools*, p. 21.

schools to which their eleven-plus performances entitled them.[1] But it is quite possible that other children are doing *less* well than they would have done in the grammar schools to which they would have won places. Also, and this is important, many of the earlier comprehensives enjoy better buildings and facilities, and above all more enthusiastic staffs than are to be found in most other schools. T. W. G. Miller remarks concerning the comprehensive schools on which his research was based that all of them were uncommonly well housed, equipped and enthusiastically staffed.[2] In 1966 more than half the full-time staff of the Inner London comprehensive schools were filling special responsibility posts.[3]

Evidence as to the comparative academic effects of streaming and unstreaming is also as yet inconclusive. The most reliable, and indeed the only extensive and up-to-date programme of research in this field is that of the National Foundation for Educational Research, of which the preliminary report on streaming is to be found in the Plowden Report. In this project the test scores of children in fifty streamed schools were compared with those in fifty schools that were not streamed. 'The overall results of the attainment testing suggest that, on the various outcomes measured, pupils in streamed schools performed better than their counterparts in nonstreamed schools. Most of the differences found were statistically significant. Few of the differences, however, were large; most amounted to less than one third of a standard deviation, and only those derived from the mechanical arithmetic score approached or surpassed half a standard deviation. In effect, what these differences mean is that, on the average, the streamed group got two or three more answers right in tests having 30 or 40 items in them. Some would consider this a small price to pay for nonstreaming if other educational and personal advantages were obtained ... The standard deviation of the test scores showed that in streamed schools there was less homogeneity in performance, and that more children in these schools were getting higher marks. There was little difference in the percentage of children scoring

[1] Ibid, pp. 97 ff.
[2] T. W. G. Miller, *Values in the Comprehensive School,*
[3] I.L.E.A., *Inner London Comprehensive Schools,* p. 36.

low marks in the two groups of schools. The most likely interpretation of this seems to be that the most able children in the streamed schools score more highly than do their counterparts in the unstreamed ones.' The report goes on to point out that the differences may not be due to streaming as such, but may be influenced by other differences between streamed and unstreamed schools – social background of the children, the greater frequency of testing and so of habituation to test situations in the streamed schools, and the attitudes of teaching staffs. Hence the authors of the report caution people against 'too much emphasis being placed on the results of this part of the enquiry. As they stand they lend small support to the controversialists on either side'.[1]

The inconclusiveness of the evidence may be thought to give some encouragement to the reformers. For the supporters of streaming are obliged to argue that it carries a great academic advantage whereas its opponents whose objections to it rest largely on different grounds, need only argue that non-streaming does no harm. If the advantages of streaming are as great as its champions maintain, one would expect this to emerge conspicuously in any tests. Perhaps both sides are right about the effects of streaming; the conservatives in arguing that in an unstreamed class the cleverest children lose by being slowed down by the pace of the duller, and the reformers in arguing that the duller children gain by the stimulation that they get from the brighter. But on balance general progress is not much affected.

The effective teaching of an unstreamed class however demands the development of informal techniques, very different from the traditional method of addressing the whole class as a body and carrying on with them a discussion in which, for various reasons, many of the children may never take part. The teacher must break the class up into groups, not necessarily the same for different subjects or at different times, and encourage each group to tackle the common syllabus in its own way and at its own level. The only class teaching takes place when the material is first introduced. Children must do a good deal of work on their own, and are

---

[1] Plowden Committee, *Children and their Primary Schools*, Vol. II, App. 11. See also Joan C. Barker Lunn, 'Streaming in Junior Schools, in *New Research in Education*, Vol. I, no. I, p. 46.

encouraged to help one another. Thus, for instance, Roy Bolam, of Abbey Wood Junior School, London, says: 'Children, like adults, learn through doing, teaching and explaining. Co-operation should therefore be encouraged . . . Able children (should) be encouraged to help others with corrections where appropriate.'[1] (This sounds like the monitor system of Victorian schools.) Peter Mauger, Head of the Nightingale County Secondary School, Wanstead, said that to facilitate the work of his unstreamed classes, children who were very backward were withdrawn from ordinary classes for a varying number of periods a day for their special needs, with a specially trained teacher. He was experimenting with bringing this teacher into the classroom to sit with backward children as required, without separating them from the remainder of the class to form a stigmatized remedial group.[2]

This style of teaching is more expensive in materials, since to work on their own, the children need 'more books, pictures, films, film strips, radio, means of duplication'.[3] It requires more planning from the teachers, and a higher standard of teaching ability. One teacher goes so far as to say, 'Must we have magicians on our teaching staffs to make non-streaming viable? I think we must.'[4] In unstreamed Inner London comprehensive schools 'Inspectors have considered the work of the departments very uneven, and this is reflected in external examination results. This unevenness is to be expected, as much depends on the skill and resources of the teacher faced with an unstreamed form.'[5]

Of special interest are the N.F.E.R.'s comments in their preliminary report on streaming: 'Streamed and non-streamed schools embody different philosophies. The streamed school seems to be more systematic in its approach, concentrates more on conventional lessons, gives more attention to the three Rs, and is likely to be more "traditional". Its staff is likely to be somewhat older and more experienced, to approve of A-stream children, of eleven-plus selection and of streaming. The non-streamed school . . . its

---

[1] R. Bolam in *Forum*, Summer 1966, p. 92.
[2] P. Mauger, 'Report of a Conference on Non Streaming', *Forum*, Spring 1960.
[3] K. R. Scott, ibid.
[4] P. Brown in *Forum*, Spring 1967.
[5] I.L.E.A., *Inner London Comprehensive Schools*, p. 62.

younger teachers hold more "permissive" views on such things as manners, noise and cleanliness; they disapprove of streaming, A-streams and eleven-plus procedures. Their teaching tends to place more emphasis on self-expression, learning by discovery and practical experience . . . The teachers in non-streamed schools *believing in streaming* obtained a higher level of arithmetical computation from their pupils, while those believing in non-streaming had fewer social isolates in the class, caused less anxiety about tests and found more of their pupils a pleasure to have in the class.'[1]

It is clear that the educational principle of desegregation does not merely involve a change in organization but a revolution in attitudes on the part of teachers so that a revolution in pupils' attitudes may follow. As Pattinson says, 'As new methods of teaching, testing and reporting were introduced individual competition was increasingly out of place . . . There are no form lists, no subject lists and neither promotion nor demotion. The School Report (form) has no provision for marks or positions . . . There are no order marks or merit marks, no detentions, no corporal punishment, prefects, or house system . . . Non-streaming is also but one important part of an organization which places a high premium on maximum personal effort, which demands high standards of self discipline and responsibility, and which regards work as good in its own right.'[2] To teach an unstreamed class well, one needs to display more alertness, and more flexibility of approach, and to manifest altogether more sympathy with individual children in their difficulties than do many teachers of streamed classes. There are assumptions that must be dropped before one can even begin on this enterprise, notably the assumption that a class must be taught as a single unit so that the teacher can initiate and control all its activities. In an unstreamed system the most proficient teachers who are in sympathy with it will be likely to teach more effectively than they ever could with streaming, and to get more satisfaction out of their work. But there will be more teachers who fail to do their job competently. Among these will be raw beginners who cannot keep order among several groups working side by side, (perhaps beginners ought not to be set to work with classes of a wide

---

[1] Plowden Report, Vol. II, p. 589.
[2] W. Pattinson, 'Streaming in Schools', *Educational Research*, June 1963.

range of ability); those who lack the qualities of personality for this sort of teaching; and those who are accustomed to formal methods and are unable or unwilling to change their ways. If these teachers are still to be employable, we should not press on too fast with unstreaming. And we are not so overburdened with teaching staff that we can afford to dispense with the unprogressive. In the light of these observations, it is all the more important that enthusiasts who have made a success of unstreamed teaching should be willing to demonstrate to the unconvinced how they set about it. Glowing accounts of the successes of unspecified methods, such as have appeared in *Forum* are unlikely to convert the doubters, who are left wondering how on earth it is all done. Anyone who discusses this matter with a mixed gathering of teachers is bound to see for himself the honest bewilderment on the faces of the uninitiated. One of the things we are not told is the maximum size of the unstreamed class that one can expect to supervise successfully. Can it be done with, say, thirty-five pupils?[1] 'The same difficulty is found with Douglas Pidgeon's suggestion for tailoring lessons to the needs of individual learners by individualized learning programmes.'[2]

The strongest resistance to comprehensivization (and *a fortiori* to unstreaming) tends to come from entrenched grammar school staffs who are inclined to believe that their academic knowledge will not be economically used in the teaching of less able children. Many of them neither like nor profess to understand this sort of child. Faced with compulsory comprehensivization, some of them will talk of leaving the profession, others will retire early, and of the remainder many may become permanently disgruntled. Yet more, and not fewer, of those capable of teaching to 'A' level will be needed in a comprehensive system.

The situation is so complex that I propose to summarize its leading features before suggesting some tentative conclusions.

On the one hand both forms of educational segregation as now practised involve the grading of children into 'better', 'not so

---

[1] For further discussion on teaching of unstreamed classes, see pp. 138-49 below.

[2] D Pidgeon, 'Learning in Secondary School', *New Society*, vol. V, June 10th 1965.

good' and 'hopeless' on inadequate grounds, too early in life, and with too little genuine opportunity for review. This is harmful to the educational progress and the attitude not only to school but to society at large of those who get into the lower grades.

On the other hand effective teaching is more difficult in classes and in schools of mixed ability. This difficulty increases as children grow older because the gap in their attainments widens. Thus unstreaming is easier in primary schools and some grouping by ability, whatever the form it takes, becomes urgent as pupils approach G.C.E. or C.S.E. level. The difficulty is also greater the greater the range of ability in a given class or school. So the un-streamed comprehensive faces the biggest problems and the adoption of unstreaming in comprehensive schools is a gamble which in some cases may turn out not to have been justified by the circumstances. Success will depend on exceptional qualities in the staff. For instance where a new comprehensive school, housed in new and well equipped buildings, is peopled beyond its first year level almost entirely by the pupils and the staffs of superseded secondary modern schools which were formerly streamed, the problems encountered in running it as a mainly unstreamed school are going to be formidable. It seems as though staff with no experience of the unstreamed situation will need in-service courses in unfamiliar techniques and the example of imported teachers who had already proved successful with unstreamed classes. The case for unstreaming is actually stronger in schools of the tripar-tite system, which have a narrower range of ability at all levels, but even here in-service training in informal methods will be needed by some of the staff.

At present most comprehensive schools are still streamed. An educational system in which *all* schools were comprehensive would get rid of the once-for-all sorting out of the eleven-plus, and the conspicuous differences in status as between grammar and modern schools; it would not necessarily eliminate selection, which might still take place within the school, but one hopes in a more flexible manner, making as much use as possible of the device of setting. The other main advantage of the bigger comprehensive is the wide range of options that it can offer.

Meanwhile nobody disputes that some children of very low

intelligence need to be taught separately in special schools. But are there enough places in such schools, and are unselected schools in a position to undertake as much remedial work as is actually needed? We do hear of teachers struggling to make provision in a thirteen-year-old class for boys and girls whose reading age is only six. At the opposite end of the spectrum are those gifted children who if they develop their full potential should be certain of university education leading to a first or a good second class honours degree. For the proper exercise and maturation of their talents they need faster and more intensive study than their contemporaries, and for them a small number of selective grammar schools would be appropriate, some of them boarding schools. Indeed, instead of increasing the numbers of our grammar schools in order to make provision for large numbers of border-line children, many of whom have no academic interests (and thus turning grammar education into a status symbol for the ordinary rather than a severe training for the exceptionally able), perhaps we should have kept the number of grammar places relatively small and reserved them for the cleverest children. There would then have been no question of every other child being expected by his parents to get into the grammar school, nor of a substantial proportion of grammar school pupils getting the advantages of better equipment and more highly qualified teachers simply because their parents could afford to pay as had previously happened. The resources which went into the additional grammar schools could more fairly have been spread over secondary education as a whole.

Having committed this original error of policy, we now find ourselves in a situation from which the best way out will very likely be to return most of the grammar schools to the common secondary pool under comprehensivization schemes, retaining only sufficient grammar schools to accommodate exceptionally able children. Most university entrants will still receive their secondary education in comprehensives.

We must not underestimate two formidable difficulties in the way of transforming the tripartite system into a comprehensive system. One is that our existing buildings are too small, and large enough sites for replacements are not easy to find in built-up areas, so that an attempt to comprehensivize quickly must involve parcelling out many a so-called comprehensive into several scattered buildings already in existence and each accommodating a limited age range. The worst effects of this arrangement are the resulting discontinuity of school experience as children graduate from one set of buildings to another, and the segregation of younger children from the company, the example and the leadership of their elders. As the Plowden Report says: 'A two year school is not educationally sound, particularly at this [11-13] stage of children's development. In the first year they will be settling down; in the second they will be getting ready to leave. There will be no time to become the school community which children of this age particularly value.'[1] The other difficulty arises from the losses implicit in the break-up of established teams of grammar school teachers who think of going into comprehensives as being demoted. However mistaken they may be on this point their attitude remains an obstacle to the smooth transition from one system to the other.

From the foregoing discussions it is clear that comprehensivization *by itself* will not completely solve the problems of giving an effective education to the rejected majority of the segregative system, and at the same time eliciting their enthusiasm for it. We have in addition to experiment with unstreaming and with the techniques relevant to it, we have to revolutionize the attitudes and approach of large numbers of teachers.

In this field interesting work is being undertaken by the Curriculum Laboratory of the University of London's Goldsmiths' College, which is concerned not only with remedying discrimination, but with finding solutions for problems such as I described in my earlier chapters – how to encourage children of all levels of ability to achieve the best understanding, within their powers, of themselves and their environment, and how to get them to co-operate creatively with others, to achieve satisfying levels of

---

[1] Plowden Report. Vol. I. paragraph 397. Perhaps it would be better to make do for the present with small comprehensives each in its separate building? The range of options would be limited but each school would have its own specialities and at the appropriate stage some pupils would choose to be transferred to another school.

aesthetic experience, and to deal intelligently with the pressures of an urbanized and rapidly changing society.

Their first pilot course for experienced teachers, concerned with the raising of the school leaving age, was held at Goldsmiths College in the spring term of 1965 and drew attention to the need for a radical rethinking of the aims and methods of secondary education. Although it would not be possible in a short exposition to do justice to all the ideas put forward in the reports of their first five pilot courses and four issues of their broadsheet *Ideas*, I shall quote some of their statements of intention, notice difficulties inherent in them and mention the ways in which they are working to meet these.

Their outstanding suggestion is for a type of curriculum suitable for unstreamed classes, starting from the actual concerns and interests of the children themselves and designed to stimulate them to work willingly and find enjoyment in the enterprise. Leslie Smith, the editor of *Ideas*, says in his summary of this 'Fourfold Curriculum'; 'Firstly, there is the *interdisciplinary enquiry* itself (IDE) which involves all pupils in the secondary school usually in their year groups; the younger pupils spending up to 50 per cent of their time on this form of activity and the older ones spending less time on IDE. Secondly there is that area of the curriculum which could be called autonomous studies, or other main studies. These studies include those subjects which teachers perceive as requiring linear treatment. Teachers vary greatly in the degree to which they see their disciplines as being in part or in full linear and progressive, and this variation has to be respected . . . Perhaps it is in this section of the curriculum that the study of languages will best take its place. Thirdly, there is that part of the curriculum which can be called remedial education, in the sense that all pupils at different times need supportive educational activities . . . all students, for instance, need a progressive reading programme. Sometimes these activities provide advanced skills; sometimes they are remedial in the customary sense; sometimes they help able pupils by providing skills which enable them to advance their performance in areas of strength. Fourthly the IDE-based curriculum would include provision for special interests: interests which would emerge from any source.

'IDE and autonomous studies would be the concern of pupils working in clusters, in the main within age-groups. Remedial education in the special sense proposed may well be the concern of year-groups of pupils but may be shared by pupils from some or all age groups in the school. The fourth group, special interests, is essentially for mixed age groups . . . This work is an important opportunity for the gifted pupil and for those with highly developed personal interests, but it also has a part to play in the encouragement of special interests of all pupils; indeed the chance to work untrammelled in this area of the curriculum may well break the log-jam of learning difficulties for some poor achievers.'[1]

The clearest statement of IDE itself comes from a pamphlet by William I. Brown and some colleagues at the Aberdeen College of Education, as quoted in this same issue of *Ideas*.[2] These people define an IDE or Inter Disciplinary Enquiry as 'a learning [process] which begins from the learner's need to explore his environment: if possible, from interests already formed . . . In pursuing this Enquiry the learner will be encouraged to use the subject-matter, and in varying degrees, the subject-manner, of a number of disciplines hitherto regarded as separate.' Pupils will 'explore their environment by asking or being prompted to ask the sort of question they are capable of asking, and being guided to find the sort of answer they can understand. What emerges then will be a pupils' synthesis from a pupils' team: and the feeling that the work has arisen largely from their own needs and interests and has been achieved by their own exploratory drives could provide a motivation which is lacking in the class teaching of imposed curricula, however skilfully these have been devised to fit general age requirements . . . Teachers should have previously explored together the various topics which could conceivably arise. Not all that has been prepared may be needed: not all that is needed may have been prepared . . . in which case, if improvisation cannot fill the gap, interest will have to be guided into a channel already dug . . . IDE is a part of school work where the pupil can most easily learn the habit of working with others and for others, since this is not a part of the work where his

[1] Leslie Smith, 'Fourfold Curriculum', *Ideas*, no. 3, p. 3.
[2] *Ideas*, no. 3, p. 8.

individual achievements have to be measured against any clearly defined general criterion of confidence. In IDE he can learn how to contribute to a group decision, how to carry out for the sake of the group that part of the group objective which he has undertaken, and how to learn from the work of others similarly done. He can learn in this microcosm how to work with initiative, but at the same time, co-operatively and responsibly, as he will have to work in the macrocosm of grown-up society . . . It is hoped that in the course of the Enquiry pupils will be encouraged to use competencies already gained . . . In so far as they are prepared to postpone the pursuit of their immediate interests to acquire the intellectual equipment for later investigations, the linear curriculum of many Certificate courses is a proper complement to IDE. Indeed we would hope that IDE served to provide sound motivation for the acquisition of new skills and a structured framework of knowledge . . .' In linear subjects, 'a skilful inclusion of connected subject matter may well reap a double benefit both to the linear subject and to the branching enquiry'. Where Programmed Learning or Language Laboratory Courses are available in linear subjects related to the IDE, the pupils need not then wait for the forming of a class in the subject.

In the same issue of *Ideas*, on page ten, appears an article by John Jones, head of the Art department, Mark House Secondary School, Walthamstow, describing an IDE enterprise on 'Europe Day', which occupied children throughout the school for a part of their time in each week of the spring term, culminating in an exhibition lasting three days and visited by all the children in form-groups completing questionnaires set by the teachers, by children from other schools, by parents and members of the public. In this same school a number of craftwork community projects also took place; the building and furnishing of a flat within the domestic science centre, the creation and equipping of a theatre in the upstairs hall (which was used for ambitious productions presented by the children and their teachers), a library carved out of a classroom, a motor vehicle maintenance shed, and an office with 'better facilities than those to be found in the head-teacher's suite'. Leslie Smith in describing these projects says that 'Project work of this type formed only a part of the programme of practical work. Each craft had its own programme of individual or group projects . . . individual pupils who wanted to take external examinations in practical subjects were able to do so within the framework of this flexible programme.'[1]

Unfortunately these are the only published examples of the IDE method in practice, and my enquiries have not elicited any others.

Finally I quote as expressing the overall intention of the IDE programme this remark of Mrs Charity James, of Goldsmiths' College, leading tutor to the pilot courses for experienced teachers: 'Our present education is an education for being a functionary, for doing what you are told, it's as simple as that; and if we want a society of people who contribute, who participate, then in their schooling they have got to be co-opted into a dynamic society, not inducted into a static one.'[2]

The role of the teachers is obviously much changed. 'For English secondary schools we see the best pattern as one in which a group of teachers, representing a group of major disciplines, should work for some 40-50 per cent of the working week across several classes of a total year-group . . . The basic working unit within the year-group would be not the class but small flexible groups of pupils, say two to seven, working together on special aspects of a common enquiry. These small groups or "clusters" are likely to include children who in a rigid system would have been relegated to different streams.'[3]

Now the first thing to be said about this new educational method is that it is setting out to do some things for children which at present are not usually being done. It is trying to develop intellectual initiative in them, in place of the readiness to be led. It is trying to foster the ability to co-operate and participate in situations of a more adult kind than the typical classroom situation (which offers little scope for moral learning). It is trying to make children see for themselves the need for the linear disciplines which when taken in isolation tend to be such drudgery. It is trying to bring about more natural and many-sided relationships

[1] Leslie Smith, 'Community Projects', *Ideas*, no. 2, p. 7. For another instance of an early IDE project (on 'Change') see *Ideas*, no. 4, p. 10 (Tom Lewis, 'Third Year Grown-ups').

[2] 'Post Conference Forum', *Ideas*, no. 3, p. 5.

[3] *Report of Fifth Pilot Course for Experienced Teachers*, p. 27.

between teachers and taught than are possible in the conventional school situation. All this and more are to be hoped for as consequences of handling unstreamed children in unconventional ways arrived at by persistent experiment, never losing sight of the goal of stimulating the individual pupil to work as near as possible to his ceiling.

It is obvious that in inefficient hands the fourfold curriculum based on IDE could be singularly unproductive; teachers and pupils could waste their time in undirected fumbling. And it is going to be impossible to assess the amount and the quality of the work done by individual pupils engaged in group enquiries. Evidence of the academic benefits of IDE have therefore to be looked for in the progress children make in their autonomous studies, which should profit from the liberative and stimulating effects of the spontaneous group projects. Clearly the four parts of the curriculum have to be kept in balance. The effectiveness of the system would need to be demonstrated through long term comparisons between the work and behaviour of pupils in schools that had adopted it and those of pupils in other schools, using progress in autonomous studies and results in Certificate examinations as the academic yardstick. *A priori* one would expect the IDE pupils to do better academically, provided that their total curriculum had been carefully balanced; but so long as their academic performance was not *worse* than that of the control group, improved behaviour and greater industry, initiative and co-operativeness would indicate the success of the scheme, which is important as an attempt at moral and social training. There will of course be the usual difficulty of making a fair comparison when teachers in schools using IDE curricula are bound to have the advantage of enthusiasm due to the novelty of what they are doing.

One is in sympathy with the desire of the Curriculum Laboratory staff to prolong IDE work by unstreamed 'clusters' if possible up to G.C.E. 'O' level stage. Charity James voices my own unspoken thought when she says: '[Today] while the lower ranks are offered, from 14–16, courses on the "humanities" or "social education", those who are being groomed to become members of an elite are not thought to need any coherent study of man and his environment. The whole caboosh is the product of a divided society, using its educational system to deepen its divisiveness. It is also the product of a society which still cannot have woken up to the need for *all* students to have an exploratory, creative and meaningful education. No one, surely, is too intelligent for that?'[1] The case for taking this line is all the stronger in that five good 'O' level passes should be enough for anyone, leaving time to spare for IDE projects of a sociological character, and in that teenagers who are motivated to work for 'O' levels are capable of covering a good deal of ground in a relatively short period and may not actually need to spend so much time preparing for their examinations as many grammar school teachers suppose. Surprisingly, nobody seems to have tried to determine the optimum times to be given to study by children of different age groups and differing levels of competence. In *Ideas*, no. 4, Leslie Smith is reported as actively engaged in trying to set up in collaboration with one of the Boards an Interdisciplinary 'O' level examination, although it is hard to see how this could be done. Charity James suggests that external examinations as set at present 'could be prepared for either in Autonomous Studies or in the Remedial Section. In fact, I would hope to see an increasing amount of preparation taking place in this Clinic (Remedial), with small groups or individual students rapidly working through programmes and assignments which would assist them to memorize the material and learn the specific skills required by conventional public examinations. This is a realistic placing of these examinations, a brisk visit to the automat and then back to one's education.'[2]

So far so good. This approach and method have to be considered seriously because of the incentives for learning and the advantages in social training that they seem to offer, and the opportunities for children to collaborate effectively with their teachers instead of dissociating themselves from them. The realization that education is a lifelong process, since even teachers in IDE are seen to be still learning, and that it really can help us to extend our interests and discover our hidden talents, would inevitably come to pupils involved in well-run IDE courses. The barriers between the education-resistant and their teachers would be eroded.

---

[1] Charity James, 'Fourfold Curriculum and R.S.L.A.', *Ideas*, no. 4, p.1.
[2] Charity James, 'Fourfold Curriculum and R.S.L.A.', *Ideas*, no. 4, p. 2.

But it would be doing a disservice to the development of IDE to pass over its difficulties lightly. When, as at present, so few teachers at secondary level are versed in the techniques of sorting pupils into viable groups and getting them to work in the manner suggested, many schools will find the IDE programme un-acceptable. The quality of the teachers will need to be uncommonly high, if order is to be maintained and a reasonable amount of work done. Any one teacher in a 'focus group' of five or six will be expected to keep his eye on up to 200 children in 'clusters' of from two to seven individuals, to keep records of whatever is done that is relevant to his own specialities, to make suggestions without forcing his own ideas on the pupils, and somehow or other to assess the work of each of them. It will tax the energy and ingenuity of a keen and talented practitioner to do all this. Will more children evade effective supervision under this system than with normal class teaching? Much depends on the organizing ability of a few people, teachers and pupils. Nor can it be taken for granted that group work will generate the warmth so often mentioned by Mrs James in her book *Young Lives at Stake*. Quite, apart from the usual quota of isolates in a class, is it not true that some groups tend to search out one or more members against whom their collective malice or resentment can be channelled? Can teachers be sure of noticing such a situation if and when it arises and tactfully removing the victim to work elsewhere? The unfair-ness of his peer group can surely be as damaging to a child as that of a teacher. I should like to be able to feel more certain that this is not a serious problem.

Nor does the pressing problem of assessment receive any con-vincing solution in Mrs James' book.[1] She points out that 'the standardized attainment tests undertaken by a year group can be a useful occasional guide to those who want a rough estimate of how their pupils' average attainment compares with the sample used in validating national tests . . . unfortunately, the standardized tests available at the moment are limited in what they test as attainment. Undoubtedly one of the tasks facing those engaged in a new and more open kind of schooling will be to engage with test and measurement experts to devise new kinds of attainment tests.

[1] Section III, Chapter 3, 'Evaluation, Appraisal and Counselling'.

Before this can be done they will need to formulate with precision the kinds of behaviours that they wish to evaluate.' (p. 167-8). While they are feeling their way towards this, they are advised to invite comments from uncommitted observers and with their help devise simple internal tests. But such tests could not reveal how the children's progress compared with that of others not using IDE methods.

Concerning the individual pupil Mrs James argues that his work should not be marked in the sense of being compared with some imaginary standard and then ranked in a form order, since this 'is to distract attention from the actual strengths and weaknesses of the work'. Mrs James believes that most school marking is badly done, tests being ill designed, and the pupil's work at the mercy of the subjective impressions of a single teacher. Pieces of work should therefore be marked by groups of teachers (though how they would find time to assess collectively every piece of work is not explained). She advocates a system of collecting the impressions of all teachers concerned with each child on a general record sheet covering all children taught by that group of teachers, in every field of behaviour on which they are to be assessed. The pupil's own view of his performances is to be taken into account. (At least then we should know what he *thought* he was doing.) The general intention is that teachers should look out for trends and changes in the performances and behaviour of pupils. This could be worth attempting, but surely not as the sole way of assessing pupils? And how is a poor devil of a teacher, faced with quite a large number of pupils, to come by reliable and recordable impressions of 'the way in which in their daily work pupils set about choosing tasks, identifying problems, planning their work, communicating their findings through various media and seeing how one piece of work leads on to others, or relates to the proceedings of other clusters of children' (p. 174)? Since 'the mass ritual of seasonal examinations' would be substituted by two case conferences a year for most children (more for some) it seems possible that the verdicts on many would be too vague to be valuable. Is this really more reliable than the mass examinations? Even given teachers who were up to the tricky work of assessment in this style, still they could only compare the records of each child with those of his fellow pupils. There would be no standard of comparison as between these and children from other schools, either individually or collectively. But prospective employers and admissions tutors to institutions of further education need at least a rough and ready indication of which applicants show more of certain sorts of ability than others. External examinations, with all their shortcomings, do furnish a guide line, indispensable when places cannot be offered to all comers. Nor would the Jamesian appraisal system enable the teachers involved to know whether IDE as a method was really effective academically, whatever its other merits. For this we need prolonged and systematic comparison between the work of IDE-trained children and others, using the yardstick of external examinations taken in the autonomous studies and remedial sectors of the IDE schools. It would also be instructive to see side by side the findings of the IDE appraisal system and those of external tests on IDE pupils, bracketed with explanations of divergences. This would give its inventors the opportunity to explain by reference to concrete instances the superiority of their method of assessment. Indeed one obstacle to the evaluation of IDE as a method by those not involved in it is the lack of examples showing how it actually works.

In the long run, IDE children need to be shown to be at least as successful academically as other children and we might expect them to be more so if the method does all that is claimed for it. If it cuts down truancy and delinquency rates in schools where it is used and engenders a tradition of co-operation, it will certainly have achieved what many schools dearly long to do. But will it do this only at the expense of academic efficiency? I feel that if it can be made to work at all well, it should be successful in all fields of school activity. But where are the teachers to be found who can operate it well? How long must we wait for descriptions of how it has worked in particular schools? In so far as it succeeds in training young people to take a line of their own, how far will it be *un*fitting them for work under today's conditions, where so much has to be done in accordance with strict industrial routines? And will the problem of appraisal be solved without recourse to external examinations?

Perhaps the greatest importance of this experimental work is as a corrective to the undue rigidity of much class teaching, curriculum-planning, testing and marking in this country. Perhaps somewhere in between the two extremes we shall find methods of teaching unstreamed classes effectively. Learning in groups of mixed ability might receive more programming from the teachers without all pupil-spontaneity being lost. In this context, the work of G. O. M. Leith and his colleagues at the University of Birmingham School of Education's National Centre for Programmed Learning is promising.[1] 'Comparisons between groups showed that heterogeneous grouping was better for both high-and low-I.Q. subjects than either homogeneous pairs or individual work'. This is exactly what we need to know about. It implies that unstreamed schools could produce better academic performances than streamed, since higher-grade children do as well unstreamed as streamed, and some lower grade children do better.

In the Post Conference Forum in *Ideas*, no. 3, Charity James says that a number of Colleges of Education are already beginning to 'see IDE as the right way of dealing with curriculum courses'.[2] But it is among experienced teachers that converts most need to be made, for it is likely to take a very experienced team of teachers to make a success of the IDE-based curriculum. Regionally-organized courses seem the obvious way of introducing it to them. Its sponsors are well aware of this. 'Unfortunately the very teachers who need this are not the most likely to attend, and so it may well be that such courses should always have as an element of their objectives assistance to members . . . in acting as change-agents in schools.'[3] In any given school 'if we bring together first a small voluntary group from the staff to discuss adolescent problems, it can as time goes by gradually assimilate more and more teachers . . . By-products of this process are many. The participants tend to have to come to terms with themselves, and learn the give-and-take of human relationship. They develop a more creative approach to their vocation, as they are necessarily more deeply involved in evaluating their work and their personal effectiveness.'

[1] e.g. R. Amaria, L. A. Biran and G. O. M. Leith, 'Individual versus co-operative learning in a secondary school', *Research Report on Programmed Learning* no. 17.

[2] Charity James, 'Fourfold Curriculum', *Ideas*, no. 3, p. 3.

[3] *Report of the Fifth Pilot Course for Experienced Teachers*, p. 68.

In connection with this difficulty of persuading experienced staff to try out new methods, it must strike anyone who talks with a cross-section of teachers from different types of school how seldom one comes across a teacher who is not deeply prejudiced in favour either of the methods and approach to which he is accustomed, or of novel methods simply because they are novel. Unconscious bias seems to be at work in preventing the old hand from perceiving much merit in the innovations, and the enthusiast-for-change from giving full weight to the difficulties arising out of the new approach. Because of this situation I have tried to review fairly all the pros and cons of educational desegregation, and I believe that I have shown how strong is the case for taking non-selection as far as is practicable, having due regard for the need to extend some pupils and equip them with the requisite range of 'O' and 'A' levels as a foundation for further education.

IX · Teachers

Beyond any doubt, the most important factor in education is the quality of the teacher. Good teachers matter more than well planned buildings or up-to-date equipment, maybe more even than the organization of the school and the methods in use. Partridge's *Middle School* was a set of well equipped buildings, and as such the pride of the city to which it belonged: it was its teachers that made of it a mediocre institution in which the duller boy (and the average one who had been unlucky enough to get into one of the lower streams) was neglected. When visiting schools one is repeatedly told that it is normally the personality of the teacher that furnishes a child's incentive to work. This statement seems to mean that neither his own curiosity nor his desire to excel nor the encouragement from his parents nor even the simple wish to keep up with his peers makes so much difference to him as his relationship with his teacher. If the teacher can get a child on the same side as himself, identifying with his values, that child will exert himself to learn. If instead the teacher 'gets across' him, awakening his hostility, contempt, distrust or indifference, the child will lose so much of his incentive to learn that only a change of teacher can be expected to restore it. Whenever a pupil does notably well in, let us say French, but notably badly in Latin, which as another language subject has much in common with it from the classroom point of view, the likely explanation is that with this child the teacher of French has succeeded whereas the teacher of Latin has failed. Given the same teacher in both subjects his performances would probably be similar in both. Instances of this sort of situation may be seen as far on as in Ordinary level results. Some lucky individuals have the gift of being able to create good relationships with their classes from the outset. Most have to learn by experience how to do it. Meanwhile the well known gap between teacher and taught appears as soon as children are put with a teacher in whom they have no confidence. Instead of persuading them to accept his values, academic, aesthetic or moral, such a teacher does harm by setting them against anything that he shows he cares about.

What sort of teachers do we need?

We need people who genuinely care for children and want to help them become competent and mature men and women, capable of enjoying their lives. (It is not necessarily the teacher who aims at keeping them happy in the classroom who is doing the best for them in these respects.) It is usual today to say that society ought not to count on men and women to dedicate themselves to teaching any more than they would to other kinds of work (and this at lower rates of pay than they could get in far less responsible jobs). As a matter of fact, we do need the dedicated types in teaching just as much as we do in medicine. We also need a vast army of staff, and to get both the quality and the numbers we are going to have to pay better, especially at the very level at which teachers are least worth what they get, that is to say, when they are beginners. We have to make the teacher once more a respected figure in the local community, as he used to be in the days before the war when working class wages were far less in relation to teaching salaries. He has to be a solid and responsible person who does not think of his job primarily in terms of good tenure and long holidays, but as a calling on which the future quality of experience in this country will depend. For well taught youngsters invest more interest and effort in their lives and get correspondingly more out of them. Since 'success' is increasingly measured by earning power in most peoples' eyes, including those of the teachers' critics, the teacher must be both well paid, and *worth* his pay.

What special qualities does a teacher need? Intelligence, ingenuity, doggedness, charity, a sense of humour, fairness, and the ability to behave equably in the face of provocation whatever his temperament.[1] Few candidates for the profession will begin with such a basketful of virtues, but many of these depend so much on habit that a determined individual can train himself to approach

[1] cf. K. L. Evans, *Educational Research*, June 1959. 'There does not appear to be any best type of teaching personality. Even poor mental health is not always a handicap.'

the ideal nearly enough for all practical purposes. When he is with a class the teacher should always be the best sort of person he is capable of being. His lapses should be reserved for some other environment. Qualities that are not appropriate in teachers are serious emotional instability leading to uneven handling of the class on different occasions so that children become confused as to what is expected of them, persistent excessive irritability, rigidity concerning methods and approaches, obvious vanity such as a class can play upon and worst of all, the tendency to dither. A certain dose of exhibitionism and bossiness is an almost inescapable occupational malady of teachers and can be turned to advantage on the job. (It is the teachers' families and neighbours who tend to suffer most!) But fundamentally what we require of a teacher is what used to be known as integrity, by which I mean the invariable practice of acting on principle instead of out of prejudice or passion.

But what sort of teachers are we actually getting?

All kinds but not nearly enough. The reason for the shortage of teachers is not so much that we are not training enough of them as that there is an abnormally high rate of wastage. Some who leave the profession are men dissatisfied with the life, the pay and the prospects, but even more are young women who after a few years marry and start having babies, and have to give up teaching. A generation back, girls' schools and primary schools were largely staffed by spinsters to whom teaching had become their whole life. Today we cannot expect the same whole-heartedness from the girls who take up teaching knowing that they will probably leave it soon. And married women teachers who return to the schools after getting their youngest into a day nursery or the reception class of an infants' school naturally find that their first priority is their own family, so that they are never as reliable as men teachers. Few married women will acquire enough seniority to take positions of responsibility in schools. Since most of our future women teachers will be either inexperienced, or married with a dependent family, we shall have to concentrate on recruiting more men. But have we enough men of suitable quality coming forward for training as teachers? So far, the answer seems to be, No. What then must we do?

At the National Union of Teachers' Conference of March 25th, 1967, the recruitment plan proposed by Sir Ronald Gould included higher salaries, bigger teacher training establishments, and the raising of teachers' status, by not permitting graduates to teach without specific training for the job nor letting unqualified non-graduates (e.g. sixth-formers) take charge of classes. Further, all local authorities should be required to employ every qualified married woman who wished to return to teaching (apparently irrespective of her past record as a teacher).

The concern of teachers with the brightness of their public image (raising of teachers' status) is understandable, if only in terms of their ability to exact respect as a body from their pupils, and their pupils' parents. And it is understandable that they should try to improve this image by insisting on the difference between the teacher who has a specific teaching qualification and the one who has not. But the general public will take little notice of the possession or non-possession of a diploma or certificate unless those who have it *are* outstandingly more effective teachers than those who lack it. Yet unquestionably there are teachers with diplomas who turn out to be lazy, indifferent to the well-being of their pupils, progress-resistant, popularity-seeking or just plain incapable of controlling a class. The training qualification is not a guarantee that its possessor will make an effective teacher. Nobody can be a good teacher until he has had a fair amount of teaching experience. Moreover, it seems doubtful whether the instructors in our colleges of education have sufficiently clear and consistent ideas as to what qualities are desirable in a would-be teacher. As Professor Frank Musgrove said in a lecture to a School Practice Study Group at the Birmingham University School of Education: 'I would like to see the validity of the criteria of teacher-effectiveness established more firmly in reason and research.' In the Manchester University School of Education's project 'To assess the effectiveness of selection, training and examining of school of education students in the light of subsequent performance', it was found that correlations between the assessments made by education and subject tutors of a student's work varied between ·23 and ·77, with a mean correlation of ·58. This being so, it is hardly surprising that some of the people who do acquire their teaching qualification prove to be unproductive teachers, who lower the status of their profession in everybody's estimation.

If the status of the profession is indeed an important factor in recruitment of suitable candidates, might we not even do better with a smaller number of teachers who were of a higher quality, were seen to be so, and could therefore be more highly paid? The prospect of joining a select group with emphasis on vocation, and a pay scale which suggests selectiveness, might attract more male candidates of the better types. This would inevitably involve the use of classroom ancillaries for jobs like marking the register, preparing and stowing away apparatus and looking after the school library, time-consuming chores which take the teacher's attention off the children and require nothing more than trained clerical ability. (One junior school head teacher went so far as to suggest that ancillaries might even hear children read, a never-ending task since each child who does not read fluently needs to be heard at least once a day; other teachers would disagree with him on the ground that this is a real teaching task which should not be assigned to the non-teacher.)

As it is, too many people opt for teaching as an occupation because they could not think of anything else to do, or because they were unable to qualify for some other calling, or because they supposed that the hours of work were short and the holidays long, or for other reasons unconnected with the hard facts of classroom life. If every candidate were clearly and challengingly told of the problems and difficulties of the profession and its many responsibilities, then some at least of the more unsuitable, notably the timorous, would be frightened off; we should not have to undertake the expense of training them when they would be unable to stand up to the job. Sir Ronald Gould at the N.U.T. conference in March 1967 pointed out that 3 out of 5 women and 1 out of 5 men are leaving teaching within 5 years of qualifying. Given a lower rate of wastage, we could manage on fewer recruits and the classroom situation would be more stable. The key to the situation seems to be an improvement in techniques for assessing both candidates and trainees.

The history of the profession in the 1930s shows that a high national rate of unemployment at that time helped to make teaching an attractive career because of its security of tenure. There were also extra allowances for those working in the same urban areas where there is now such a struggle to man the classrooms. Many head teachers in the schools of such areas today are men and women who came there as newly qualified teachers during that heyday of recruitment for the education authorities of the big cities. But with their present day junior staff it is quite a different story. These are always on the move. They are discontented, thinking of leaving because some other education authority or some other occupation tempts them. Security of tenure means less to them than it did to their predecessors. They want to earn more, and this is not sheer greed. Their basic difficulty is the cost of housing in areas where the local authority refuses to provide accommodation for young teachers. Although the neophyte teacher's wife may also go out to work (frequently as a teacher herself), her earnings are not taken into account by Building Societies as a basis for repayment of loans and so the couple find themselves unable to borrow all they need to buy and furnish a house. They have to spend so heavily on private lodgings that the possibility of a house of their own recedes into the far future. Not surprisingly, as soon as they can they move into jobs with a local authority which does supply accommodation at subsidized rents, allowing them to save for their own house in the not-too-distant future. And local authorities which do not offer council flats to their teaching staff still wonder why they experience such a shortage of applications for their posts! The usual excuse for not thus housing teachers, even the younger ones, is that all the other municipal employees would expect like concessions, and the housing queue would become more unmanageable than ever. To this the reasonable reply is that if education is to get the priority it sorely needs in our society, we may have to relieve young teachers of their housing worries before we consider the needs of clerical assistants at the council offices or workers in the motor industry.

In trouble over housing, perpetually short of money, the married male teacher at the beginning of his career is often a shabby dresser with a beat-up old car or none at all. He accepts evening class teaching and weekend jobs to cover the costs of the baby, and all this lessens the amount of vitality he can give to his main job. His pupils notice his seediness as contrasted with the sharp dressing of his contemporaries who are getting big money in the motor industry. This hardly adds to the lustre of the professional image. Financially the present is not seductive. He will need to look to the future for the inducements of extra allowances to departmental heads or for other special responsibilities, and hope in the end to win through to the headship of a school. The minds of some young teachers seem indeed to be far more set on ways and means of realizing such ambitions than on what they could do for their charges.

But pay and housing troubles are not the only causes for complaint among young male teachers. They and their junior women colleagues undoubtedly get a raw deal from many headmasters who turn over to them those classes that nobody else wants to take. Thus although the lower streams stand in need of firm handling and the reassuring presence of a permanent class teacher, in fact they often get a succession of temporaries and uneasy beginners, a situation in which nobody is happy. And the harder such a class makes it for the beginner, the likelier they are to lose him or her very quickly, whether to another school, another district or another occupation. The case is strong for entrusting lower streams to none but experienced teachers, who can keep order and in addition ensure that effective work is being done. It should not be regarded as beneath the dignity of a senior man to work with lower streams. The subject specialist particularly should spend some of his time with every type of stream, and should not see himself mainly as a coach for external examination candidates. These considerations strengthen the case for unstreaming, in which there are no bottom streams to be dumped on beginners and no top streams to be the prerogatives of senior staff. Where there is streaming, perhaps middle streams should be allocated for preference to beginners and regular work with lower streams should be made more palatable by payment of a special allowance.

Special allowances for various reasons are an important feature of the school situation. Our competitive system of education applies to teachers as well as children. 'Teachers may be streamed, no less than pupils'[1], and compete with one another for promotion. This no doubt is a stimulus to effort and enterprise (if indeed we can be confident that the rewards usually go to the best teachers: at least one ground for a special allowance, namely the possession of a degree, with the disagreeable distinction between higher and lower classes of degree, is unrelated to teaching performance). But the most disturbing effect of all this is the impetus that it adds to a teacher turnover which even without it would be high enough on account of women leaving to have babies, and beginners leaving because they cannot get a grip. The worst effects of this general post are to be seen in schools of the under-privileged areas, but it is to be hoped that the recently inaugurated special allowances for working in under-privileged areas will help to stabilize their teaching staffs. Surely the pay structure ought to be re-designed to encourage teachers to stay in one school long enough to reach their maximum value, which depends a good deal on their familiarity with the customs and background of the children and the methods of their colleagues. As it is, many head teachers spend too much time and energy in worrying about staffing problems and in trying to procure enough special allowances to keep their abler teachers. The common-room companionship and advice from older staff which beginners often get in a typical rapid-turnover school are hardly inspiring, and in many cases contribute to decisions to leave the profession.

Too often, 'On leaving the college, the new teacher finds himself isolated by virtue of the desperate demands made on him. He is rarely given the opportunity of working a theme to its conclusion or of relating day-to-day activities to his current interests. This can lead to a kind of alienation . . .'[2] The Head who allows neophyte teachers in his school to have experiences like this deserves at least part of his own high staff turnover, for he has failed to back up his newcomers and give them every possible inside tip, every means of strengthening their confidence, and in effect has shut them in with particular groups of children to make their way as well as they can. It is indeed mostly from the complaints of younger

---

[1] *Plowden Report,* Vol I, para, 816.
[2] *Goldsmiths College First Pilot Course for Experienced Teachers,* p. 23.

teachers with so many causes for discontent that the unattractive professional image is derived.

The happy school is that in which a head teacher with real gifts of leadership has gathered around him a devoted staff. This can happen in any sort of district. It is especially to be desired in the under-privileged areas, where it is a necessary condition of the school's being transformed into the local centre for community life, a redeeming feature in an otherwise depressing place. With a teaching team which remains relatively constant, most of the staff are widely known throughout the school's catchment area and in turn know the families, so that as each child enters the reception class he can to a considerable extent be placed and understood from the start. Indeed such schools have to guard against the build-up of prejudice among their teachers against certain families, or children from certain streets. A lively Third Session of evening activities, from supervised homework to all manner of hobbies can grow up, and I visited one where social evenings for parents have had a great success and over eighty parents at a time are turning up on two nights of the week. It is a school where obviously many people care about the well-being of young and old alike and the spirit of a community is being reborn, amid the mean streets with their blue brick pavements and scattered factories. Every child is given a booklet summarizing the organization, staff, facilities and objectives of the school, with great emphasis on courtesy and co-operation. For parents there is an additional duplicated hand-out of information so that they may understand what is being attempted in school, and spring and autumn newsletters keep this up to date. It is clear that the heavy evening programmes for pupils, their parents and the weekly recreative evening for teenagers, allied to the school clubs, could not be carried on without the voluntary help of both staff and parents. And somebody must have worked hard to make a success of the inclusion in the fourth year syllabus of golf and pony trekking! The basis of the friendly atmosphere is claimed to be the sociometric grouping of the class units, which are unstreamed but setted from the second year in English, mathematics and science. To obtain the sociometric groupings, before they leave primary school the boys and girls are asked to name the friends with whom they would most like to work and class units are assembled from the charts of these preferences. From time to time there has to be adjustment and difficult customers are tactfully dispersed among the classes. Another aspect of the social training appears in the use of the gymnasium in certain periods by children from the infants school who not only profit by the superior equipment but also experience 'the environment they hear so much about from their brothers and sisters. It is also hoped that they will lose a certain amount of the fear which they often show towards the bigger boys and girls' (*Handout for parents*).

This same school is well to the fore with activities suggested in the Newsom Report. It is of course far from being the only one in the Birmingham area where an energetic and generous staff make it possible to put on a solid evening programme of leisure time activities for pupils and ex-pupils. It is probably more satisfactory thus to integrate the evening class work that is centred on hobbies with the programme of a school which aims at being a neighbourhood social centre, than to hive it off into Evening Institutes which function separately, albeit on school premises. Many youngsters, and certainly their parents, would not consider joining classes in an Evening Institute where they did not know the staff, the lay-out of the building (which can be puzzling for strangers as I have discovered when tutoring Extra-Mural classes housed in them) or their fellow students. But a club, group or class meeting in their own school is different; the less brilliant the boy or girl the more he prefers what is already familiar. And then the informal atmosphere of the school's own evening activities is more encouraging. But to what extent should staff be expected to give up their own free time unpaid to these evening ventures?

So, gradually, in some districts there is beginning to be a return to the older set-up in which part of the feeling of belonging to the place was ascribable to the relationship between the family and the school. If this movement spreads, there will be less rootlessness within the catchment areas of such schools. The headmaster can be a sort of general father to his 'manor', and his more permanent staff can become well known local figures even though they may not live there, standing features in a landscape where too many things are changing all the time. They should all of them be something more than 'Oh, him' (or 'her') to the parents.

But this raises the interesting question of the extent to which a teacher can also be expected to function as a social worker. Teachers are not trained to be social workers. They lack the background knowledge that social workers acquire during their training and their daily work, they are used to dealing with youngsters rather than with adults. The headmistress of one inner ring school whose husband was warden of a community centre told me that in practice, whereas social workers on occasion had been able to take over and handle classes in her school, teachers who tried their hands at counselling or at organizing activities in the community centre were on the whole not successful. Teachers so easily develop a forceful 'Let Me Tell You' manner which alienates adults. If it is felt that there must be social work done inside a school, it seems most fitting that a professional social worker should be attached to a school or group of schools, having access to their files on pupils and their families, in order to deal with the stubborn problem cases which now soak up too much of the time of the headmaster and existing staff.

Once more we come back to the duties of the headmaster. A Head seems to be encouraged to do everything except teach (apart from those periods when staff shortages or illnesses make it necessary for him to deputize in the classrooms). He is organizer, public relations officer, chief disciplinarian and amateur probation officer, but rarely *head teacher*. I have yet to come across a handbook on the duties of heads. One of them said to me that nobody had ever told him what he was supposed to do: he had simply been ushered into his sanctum and left to get on with it . . . whatever 'it' was. Since less than eighteen months from the day when he said this to me, he was moving elsewhere after a painful period of floundering along on bad terms with staff and parents (being utterly opposed to the methods which had been used in the school before his appointment, but incapable of putting forward a clear alternative policy that would work), he makes an object lesson in the futility of putting a man or woman in charge of a school without instructing him about his duties. Perhaps the theory is that while he was a deputy he was learning to be a headmaster.

If so, then some head teachers are not taking seriously the task of training their deputies. Some are too old or too new, or too indifferent. Why do we not have short courses for newly appointed head teachers and for deputies too?

Such a course would be in effect a management course covering every aspect of school organization, curriculum, time-tabling, discipline, public relations and the pros and cons of educational policies. It would include genuine philosophy of education as well as ways and means. By 'philosophy of education' I do not mean the discussion of theory of knowledge, but of the function of the school within society. The purpose of the course would be to ensure that no new headmaster enters his room for the first time feeling uncertain of his aims and duties, or liable to allow some one or two aspects of school work to monopolize his attention. The great power of the head teacher in his own school has as its concomitant grave responsibilities which some neglect out of ignorance, a few from idleness or self-interest, but many because of bees in their bonnets.

In his own school the headmaster is absolute ruler like a captain on his ship. He stamps his pattern on it and sets its tone. It is his personality, his beliefs and tastes which determine the respective emphases placed on academic work, sports, practical courses, extra-curricular activities, experimental programmes or work for external examinations. There is no national programme that he must adhere to, much less a series of approved curricula. He may be a zealot for the recommendations of the Newsom or Plowden committee (according to the age groups in his school) or he may be a reactionary who relies on corporal punishment to keep order and treats children like units to be processed, rather than individuals whose development is to be assisted. The head of a primary school may be either besotted with eleven-plus results, or too much in love with the happy atmosphere he is creating to bother about the children's academic progress. Provided he can make the necessary arrangements and raise the money to finance them, he is virtually free to lay on anything that he can argue is of educational value. The notion of educational value has sometimes been very much stretched. Under the present system of schools inspection, a school due for a full inspection is always given long notice enabling it to disguise some of its practices or replace them temporarily by those known to be approved by the inspectors. Visitors can be held captive by a talkative headmaster in his room or shown only such classrooms as he would like them to see. So it comes about that the local education authority can be radically mistaken about the relative value of the work in many of its schools. A canny headmaster may be highly thought of when in fact his school is squandering the opportunities provided by modern equipment and premises. It is not that such head teachers are necessarily short on good intentions. Rather they tend to take a limited view of the policy appropriate to their school and, by various ploys and specialities, to distract attention from the narrowness and shallowness of the learning experiences that it provides for its pupils.

Quite different pictures of the same school can often be obtained from its head and different members of his staff. Because objective methods of measuring results are hard to find it is not always possible to recognize which of the pictures is truest to life. Of course inspectors of schools have enough experience to be able to recognize by quite small indications the level of efficiency of any school. But do administrators and education committees draw on their knowledge in arriving at decisions? Perhaps on the whole the consensus of opinion among his staff over the years is the best indication of a head teacher's merit. Of course no head teacher will please all of his staff. If he bends over backwards to keep them all in good humour, effectively he will not be head but simply a focus for pressure groups, a party leader more influenced by Gallup polls than by the need for an effective line of policy. Nevertheless if his staff turnover year after year is well above average for a school of its type, his efficiency or his personality must be strongly suspect. A sound man will contrive to hold some staff besides those with special allowances who cannot leave without risking a fall in income. His policy will be one which attracts and keeps teachers who want to work on his principles, even though it may sometimes mean earning a little less than they might get in another school. (There is the case of the man who gave up expenditure on smoking so that he could afford to remain with one headmaster.) Is there not something wrong with a pay structure which works against the preservation of strong long-term teaching teams led by keen and attractive top men?

The good headmaster keeps abreast of change and experiment in the educational field; he knows what is going on and applies new methods whenever he sees from reports on research that they have been justified. On the other hand, he is unwilling to turn his school into a laboratory where defenceless children are used as guinea-pigs, unless he can be assured that the research is being done in a responsible manner. (One hears of headmasters who undermine the work of entire schools by trying out in rapid succession practically every new method which has gained attention during their term of office, and manage to leave covered with glory for bigger and newer schools before the effects have caught up with them.) Nor does the good head teacher refuse to allow of any change in approach without clearly stating his objections and being open to conviction. He spends some time each week in teaching, which keeps him in touch with work at the classroom level and never loses sight of the difficulties of his junior staff as they struggle towards domination of their classes and effective lesson planning. They have a right to expect help from him and from all their senior colleagues until they are safely established. A teacher's first class can be as tricky for him to handle as a woman's first baby is for her. A head teacher who habitually leaves the weaker and the more obstreperous classes to temporary staff and novices may be suspected of having lost interest in children. Part of his job is the fostering of continuity and security, in chaotic lives.

The ingenuity of some head teachers is truly amazing. Their devices for raising money and equipment, their connections with local employers and with the police, their schemes for keeping track of what goes on on their premises,[1] their enquiries into home backgrounds, their sociometric experiments, their efforts to follow up every sort of interest in their pupils, really merit a book to themselves. Headmasters among themselves probably do not talk freely enough about their various devices nor visit one another's

---

[1] One headmaster switched on an intercom apparatus in his room and invited me to listen to what was happening in any classroom. He suggested that batches of trainees could be instructed with the help of this device.

schools. Their staffs, unless they attend courses and conferences, find themselves shut into the life of one school without opportunities for finding out what actually goes on in others. Yet they do manifest a considerable appetite for such information.

It is obvious that only an ambitious person will ever become head teacher of a city school. Most of them are genuinely keen on their work so that talking with them is an enlivening experience. Unfortunately the system of appointment by committees on which there are too many laymen gives scope to calculating careerists who are adept at catching the committee's eye. So the best of teachers is unlikely to get to the top without acquiring some skill in self-advertisement. How many of those on educational selection committees really know what will be required of an applicant for a job when he comes to grips with the problems of that particular school? And, what is even more difficult, how many of them are capable of assessing each candidates's potential for solving the problems? Sometimes one of the right men or women is appointed, occasionally The Right One, sometimes a clever fake who is incapable of doing the work but once appointed is irremovable (except on grounds of some moral misdemeanour that he is not in the least disposed to commit). It is this sort of appointment which increases the bitterness of the disappointed rivals and makes many senior teachers disillusioned and obstructive. Is there really no more reliable way of selecting the people who are to occupy posts of such responsibility?

A headmaster during his term of office has, if he cares to wield it, power to modify the educational experiences of thousands of children. Some he can condemn to neglect and delinquency while at the same time he is pushing forward borderline cases into acquiring, by the skin of their teeth, qualifications for work which they ought not to attempt (this is the extreme statement of the policy of neglecting D streams in order to cram A streams). He can transform the social life of pupils and parents and revive hope in gloomy places. He can ensure that the bright child gets his chance by persuading the parents to co-operate with him. He can make his school a centre specializing in rural science or in preparation for entry into the building trades. He can run a keen school in which almost every child makes progress, or a slack one in which his deputy wrestles with the work of two, whilst he himself functions as a J.P. or sits in his study writing a book or running a business enterprise on the side. He can be always around poking into corners, or shut away in solitary state. He may be bogged down in detail or a wonderful organizer with an eye for essentials.

Whatever the course he follows, in practice there is nobody to exercise checks over him. But there should be some way of operating a watch-dog system over head teachers. Admittedly every headmaster must be free to run his school as he thinks fit, if programmes are to be flexible enough to leave scope for experiment and for the exploitation of local and individual strengths. Still, there should be ways of detecting an idle, incompetent or downright cranky headmaster and rebuking him, or in the last resort, dismissing him. This would involve school inspections *at short notice* which were genuine fact-finding exercises. One is tempted to speculate on the effects of large pay differentials between head teachers, deputies, and the remainder of their staff: is it wise to tempt in this way people to whom a big income may be more important than the well-being of their charges? And is it altogether reasonable to make the head teacher's salary depend on the number of children in his school (thus encouraging people to switch from school to school in pursuit of the best pay), if what we really want is to promote stability among staff? And why do we pay the administrator more highly than the teacher, so that the man who wants to reach his maximum must progressively change over from teaching into organization? Perhaps head teachers, like Plato's guardians, ought to be dedicated people leading austere lives, certainly not glossy business types who belong to the Freemasons and would sooner be associated with the right people than keep up with recent educational developments. The spinster headmistress comes nearest to the Platonic picture but soon, alas, we shall see the last of her.

In sum, I have met many excellent Heads and a few dubious ones. What has most struck me is the unchecked power of each Head in his school and the chanciness of the system of promotion. Ought we not to be enquiring into ways of improving selection procedures, of preparing successful candidates for their work and of keeping them under more effective supervision? For in practice it is the Heads of schools who collectively determine the country's educational policy.[1]

I have already discussed several of the reasons why we have difficulty in recruiting and holding young teachers . . . low pay rates in the earlier years on the job, housing troubles, and an undue proportion of the awkward teaching assignments without enough help from older colleagues. It is clear that the novice does not have an easy time. But is there not more to be done in training to improve his prospects of quickly getting a grip on a class, so that interest in the work will tide him over the breaking-in period? I have met few young teachers who feel that their training has been as adequate as it might have been. Complaints are many and widely ranging. The commonest was insufficiency of school practice. This is not easy to deal with, for schools cannot be over-run with students on practice. Head teachers as well as trainees suggested sandwich courses and in-service training to replace the more normal block practice period which many trainees and young teachers said they had not been well enough prepared to profit by. Lectures in child psychology, theory of learning and classroom methods should alternate with school practice so that trainees can see for themselves instances of what they have heard about before they have time to forget it. How much do graduate students in short diploma courses actually hear about classroom problems and from whom? The raw beginner needs to be able to handle his routines smoothly and confidently, without such hesitations as are marked and exploited by a class out for diversions. How often is there effective training in the shock tactics needed for dealing with really difficult youngsters, and instruction on how to detect and neutralize potential troublemakers? A class that has no tiresome child in it must be unusual; some of these raise trouble out of all proportion to their numbers if they are not handled firmly from the outset. There can hardly be too much briefing of trainees for the task of diagnosing and dealing with problem children. It

[1] It has recently been suggested that in place of permanent Head teachers, schools should be administered by committees of senior staff with rotating chairmanships. This would take care of many of the difficulties I have mooted and would also lessen the amount of teacher-turnover.

must be sounder to arrive in the classroom well primed with
techniques that others have already found effective, than to fall
back in disorder when confronted with exhibitionists and those
who simply do not like school or teachers. All trainees today need
instruction concerning the backgrounds, attitudes and classroom
behaviour of the various immigrant groups as well as those of white
children. Trainees, I find, are often much agitated by the question
of discipline, without quite realizing that this will be solved by
coolness, conviction and know-how. Somebody has to put them
on the lines of knowing how. R. Farley, when he wrote *Secondary
Modern Discipline*, was evidently convinced from his own experiences that there existed numbers of young teachers who came
out of training ignorant of the disciplinary problems and the
techniques that he described. It may be that one reason why these
problems are not given so much prominence in training courses
is that few of the lecturers have successfully coped with *really*
difficult classes. Perhaps this weakness could be met by putting
on occasional talks by successful teachers from turbulent areas.
Lacking this type of formal instruction, the novice has to fall
back on *ad hoc* hints from colleagues, not always amounting to
much more than tips for keeping them quiet.[1] Sometimes he
reacts by regarding much that he heard whilst in training about
child-handling as irrelevant to the actual job. But he should have
been so equipped that he could walk into a room full of aggressive
youngsters knowing what approach they are most likely to
respond to.

The gap between theory and practice appears very clearly in the
matter of corporal punishment. Today hardly any theorist will
countenance it. But the N.U.T. has so far refused to condemn it.
Clearly there are a vast number of teachers who have not learned
how to cope without it, at least as a last resort. Many of them
refuse to believe that it can be dispensed with, and perhaps it
cannot unless there is an accompanying change in the outlook and
methods of the teachers. But whatever the methods it must be
remembered that a control of a class which is so complete as to

---

[1] A disquieting comment from numerous heads to whom I put the question
was that they doubted whether as many as 30 per cent of their existing staffs were
fit to serve as examples to trainees.

appear unnecessary is always the fruit of much experience, depending on the teacher's ability as a leader and his skill in tactful intervention before explosive situations develop.

In their advocacy of new informal methods of teaching some lecturers at colleges of education fail to impress on their students that to begin with they are bound to encounter difficulties in using these methods with large and restless classes, which may already have been seriously mishandled. It would seem realistic to instruct trainees to make a beginning with older and more formal methods until they felt sure of their class. It is always easier to relax discipline gradually once it has been achieved than to struggle for it after a lax beginning. A class divided into groups is always more difficult to oversee than either a class taught as a unit or one in which children are working individually. What sounds so easy and exciting in the lecture-room may well turn out to be full of pitfalls when attempted in the classroom. If it does not arouse interest in the first few minutes, the beginner's carefully prepared lesson may never get off the ground: has he the insight and the courage to abandon the programme and do something else?

Almost everyone comments on the great educational conveyor-belt which carries young people from school by way of university and/or college of education back to another school, this time as teachers, without their ever having had more than the occasional experience, in vacation jobs, of the working world outside. One wishes it were possible to rely on every entrant to the profession's having done such vacation work. Some people feel so strongly about this matter that they suggest a compulsory break in the cycle. They admit that there is a risk that when the would-be teacher has got away he may not come back. Yet something of the kind is needed if teachers are to appreciate more of the background of their pupils and the working lives that await them. Perhaps it should take the form of an occasional sabbatical term when the teacher is seconded to industrial or public service employment. This suggestion was put forward by a large seminar group of teachers of all ranks that I have been running. These same people showed a deep unsatisfied need for refresher courses, of which the local university's School of Education was never able to put on enough, because of lack of resources. Moreover they said that they wanted informal discussion groups similar to this one, in which they could talk over their problems with staff from other schools without the fear that what they had said would be reported back to the Education Office. Many mentioned the impossibility of ever seeing or hearing other teachers at work, in order to learn from their example. Shut in with his pupils, the individual teacher may have no chance to compare his methods with those of others, or to assess the value of the ideas he is working with. Under these conditions it is easy to get into ruts. The sabbatical course, or the spell of work outside teaching would put an end to staleness and inject fresh ideas. Making something of this nature a regular feature of teachers' working lives might also help to brighten the public image of the profession and raise its status, inasmuch as many of the public think of teachers as a group of people who are unattractive largely because they lack experience outside the educational world. That this view is a parody of many teachers' lives is irrelevant as long as it continues to be widely held.

What I have said about the problems of teacher-turnover in schools and loss of personnel from the profession because of poor pay in the early years, housing difficulties, the dumping of awkward classes on beginners, and childbirth, are matters of common knowledge among teachers, although it is doubtful whether the general public realize the full extent of the staffing problem. Many still dismiss teaching as an easy job and teachers as a set of moaners whose complaints are not justified. My comments on head teachers are the outcome of a series of school visits, most of them lasting all day, in the course of which I had ample opportunities to observe the personalities and methods of the head teachers; as far as I know nobody has done research on the behaviour of heads any more than anyone has produced a Handbook for Head Teachers. This field seems to be unexplored and likely to remain so unless some H.M.I. draws on his experience for publishable material. Yet as I observed, it is the heads of schools who between them determine England's school education policies. What I have put forward concerning the training and classroom problems of beginners in the profession is, I submit, worth taking seriously because it is based on the criticisms of numerous student teachers,

12

qualified teachers and head teachers, and there was so much consensus of opinion in this that it can hardly be dismissed as mere hearsay. If anyone cares to do research into the views taken by a cross section of qualified teachers on the training they have received and its relevance to their actual work in the classroom, some interesting points should emerge and I believe it would be found that the practices of *some* training institutions are somewhat lacking in realism.

X · In Conclusion

I have covered a good deal of ground. I have described the pressures of our society, the effects they may be expected to have on people, and some of the measures that I feel should be undertaken in schools as a matter of urgency to equip our young to stand up to these pressures and still lead satisfying lives. I feel now that it would be useful to summarize my own main points.

Our society is increasingly an overcrowded one, with diminishing living-space for almost everybody; at the same time, because of the growth of traffic, we make less use of the streets as extensions to private living-space. It follows that educational premises, with their playgrounds and sports fields, are important as never before as places where youngsters have room to move freely. The child from a cramping environment is likely to prove either restless and inconveniently boisterous when let loose, or at the opposite extreme, under-exercised and flabby. We are rearing a generation who lead over-sedentary lives. Nor is there room in small dwellings for the pursuit of hobbies requiring space. As palliatives for this situation I suggest larger school premises in general and roomy nursery schools for the children of cramped environments so that the habit of free movement can be begun early in life. Perhaps we should also begin to put stronger emphasis on the need for walking as a therapy. I also see an urgent need to encourage in young people a wide variety of interests which make little call on the use of space, such as reading, music, board games, photography, theatre and cinema, knitting and embroidery. It is the aesthetic interests which need to be stimulated by every means at our disposal, for these are the outstanding examples of pursuits which can give intense pleasure within a limited space. Many people who do not progress from the enjoyment of entertainment to the appreciation of art are failing to grow up and make the most of their own capacities. We also need to train children in the habit of thinking of the effects on other people of their own behaviour, for the closer people are packed together, the more they affect one another's lives. Even the lack of privacy in over-crowded residential districts must have its effect, by limiting the spontaneity of those who feel that they must be seen to be living either exactly like all the others or defiantly otherwise.

The noise and the general over-stimulation characteristics of town life are tiring in themselves, and make the essential habit of concentration difficult to form. The outcome is the 'butterfly mind'. In schools accordingly we need to keep down the level of sound, to provide quiet supervised rooms for homework and to train children to persist in anything that they seriously under-take, and not allow themselves to be distracted.

Another effect of urban life is the cutting off of people from other living things. This deprives them of a source of deep enjoyment, and prevents them from grasping that they are them-selves part of the order of nature. Seeing oneself as a part of that Whole is a vital source of religious feeling in an over-secularized society. We have therefore to keep up our efforts to bring children into contact with natural phenomena by way of a school garden and pets, visits to parks and the countryside, and exercises in weather-recording as well as lessons on the importance of weather-phenomena both geographically and socially.

The increased pace of technical change means that everyone should have some training in the use of simple tools, something of the craftsman outlook, and as far as possible, an understanding of the basic principles of electrical and mechanical phenomena as they affect the devices we use in the home and at work. In these ways young people can be at least partially prepared for their work and given a good start with do-it-yourself. The pace of technical change means, too, that most people will either have to change their jobs altogether or to take refresher courses in new techniques at some point in their lives. We need an adaptable populace, quick in the uptake. For this reason above all, it is important to strengthen the tuition in the three Rs, which should be mastered by every child who is not very dim before he leaves primary school; to emphasize attentiveness and accuracy; and (what I believe has never so far been attempted in school) to give regular exercise in factual inference. The need for this last is obvious in view of the unnecessary blunders made by almost everyone through failing to observe what is relevant to his interests and other people's, and to infer from his observations their consequences. We do not teach children to think round things nearly enough. To my mind, this is the most striking omission in our educational programmes. It does not call for special textbooks or syllabuses, nor indeed for any modification of a school's timetable, but simply for the introduction of factual inference games throughout ordinary lessons.

Social changes which affect most of us include higher geographical mobility, which brings about the well-known effect of rootlessness. To deal with this children must be encouraged in school to co-operate with one another instead of competing, each aiming at bettering his own past performances rather than some other child's. Group project work is the obvious method to be used. Face to face in the course of planning it children learn to take a realistic view of one another, to make the best of difficult partnerships and to further a joint enterprise instead of withdrawing each into his own citadel. Whenever the opportunity occurs we must make the point that friendships worth having exact effort and sacrifice, and that those who will have nothing to do with effort or sacrifice are likely to lead lonely lives. Oracy turns out to be an indispensable tool for the making of real contacts and prevention of misunderstandings, for people who are unable to communicate freely are cut off from one another even within married life. Schools by 'socializing' children can equip them to take root wherever they go.

The changing roles of women and men respectively I have discussed at length, pointing out that more and more married women will go out to work, regarding themselves as equal partners with their husbands in the provision and maintenance of the home. To ensure fairer division of labour in this situation, boys will need domestic training in school; shorter working hours in industry should leave time for both sexes to share in the housework and still have ample leisure. Schools could help to modify the obsolete views of male prerogative often inculcated by boys' own mothers. Another feature of the changing position of women is their greater sexual freedom which today carries with it much self-centred heedlessness of consequences. Here we should be pressing teenagers to look steadily at the facts; they need specific information on the difficulties of unmarried mothers and the misery of unwanted children.

I have tried to give an unbiased account of the domestic and cultural backgrounds of coloured children in our schools, and the special features they present as pupils. The published literature of the subject is largely devoted to the techniques of teaching them English, although there is plenty of other research in progress. But trainee teachers ought already to be receiving full briefing on the techniques of controlling them and helping them towards integration here. I have argued that unless we want to duplicate in England the unfortunate situation prevalent in the U.S.A., we shall need to adopt a constructive programme of housing and employing white and coloured people of similar qualifications side by side. To this end we should be promoting in school the pooling of information on their respective ways of life by the various ethnic groups. Many of the coloured youngsters will need to try harder to come to terms with life as it is lived here. In some ways it is a misfortune that their arrival in such numbers coincided with a period of unusual fluidity in our own values; this makes it much more difficult for them to find out what they should do in order to be accepted. Teachers with a real understanding of the position could make big contributions to the lessening of friction between the races, for their own attitudes influence their pupils whether they realize this or not.

On the vexed question of educational selection, it is inevitable that candidates for external examinations leading to professional training should have some courses of their own, which implies a certain amount of selection in the later stages of schooling. The vital decision is how early, how complete and how inflexible such selection need be. On grounds both of fairness and of its psychological effects, any form of selection which finally classifies large numbers as inferior (often while they are still in junior school) must be avoided. This type of segregation would be easier to justify if a marked academic advantage could be shown to follow from it, but this is not the case. By comprehensivizing and unstreaming we hope to improve the prospects of the majority who were formerly rejected and at the same time to give a richer and more realistic training to all. Some of the methods lately suggested for bringing this about show promise. Yet they are unlikely to be easy to apply, and many teachers will need a measure of retraining.

The most influential factor in education being the teacher himself, it is important to improve techniques of assessment for would-be trainees and for novice teachers. Easing the lot of the novice would contribute to solving the problem of too much teacher-turnover, but we might also consider some deceleration of the rat-race among staff. Should we be satisfied with a system of promotion which involves so many teachers in a general post? Both head teachers and their deputies need short training courses to prepare them for their work, and in view of the power exercised by head teachers we should find a way to assess their competence and if necessary limit their powers.

Being myself outside the schools system, I have felt free to tackle some topics from which teachers and educationists generally shy. Perhaps I may be allowed a few personal comments. The amount of experiment in our schools and the degree of variation from one to another are not without disadvantages: they increase the problems of adaptation for the many children and teachers who, for whatever reason, find themselves changing schools. Nobody can just drop easily into place. And when a headmaster with one set of ideas is replaced by a new man with another set of ideas, there can be considerable dislocation in the work of the school. Are we approaching the point at which we need careful assessment of the alternative styles of curriculum and teaching methods, with a view to consolidating the ground that has been gained, and identifying mistaken practices? Otherwise can we be certain that we are doing anything more than promoting a series of educational fashions? Another point is that in our insistence on child-centred education, we may have been making the job too difficult for the average teacher. Expected to employ methods that he does not properly understand, at the same time he experiences uncertainties about values. All day long he may be playing it off the cuff. We cannot expect him to be either a moral or an intellectual giant. Many still seem to be looking for guidance on what they ought to be doing and why, and what may be counted as a reasonable degree of success for them.

Why do I call the English 'uneducated'? Because, to judge from their performance, we have not noticeably succeeded in inducing them to think round the predicaments in which they find themselves, nor in training them to care about the effects of their actions on others, nor in making them eager to increase the range of their aesthetic experiences. People who leave school believing that education for them is at an end cannot be said to have even begun their education. My use of the term is harsh, yet how else can I draw attention to the disparities between what so many grow up to be and what they might have been?

Reading List

BLAKE, J. *Family Structure in Jamaica*, 1962.
BLYTH, W. A. L. *English Primary Education*, 1965.
BOLAM, R. in *Forum*, summer 1966.
BROWN, P. in *Forum*, spring 1967.
BURGIN, T. and EDSON, P. *Spring Grove*, 1967.

CLARKE, H. The Effects of a Candidate's Age, in *The British Journal of Educational Psychology*, Vol. XXVI, part 3.
CURRICULUM LABORATORY OF GOLDSMITHS COLLEGE, UNIVERSITY OF LONDON. *Ideas*, a broadsheet published at intervals.
CURRICULUM LABORATORY OF GOLDSMITHS COLLEGE. *Pilot Courses for Experienced Teachers*, Reports 1–5.

DOUGLAS, J. W. B. *Home and School*, 1964.

EVANS, K. L. in *Educational Research*, June 1959.

FARLEY, R. *Secondary Modern Discipline*, 1960.
FITZHERBERT, K. West Indian Children in London, in *Occasional Papers on Social Administration* (edited by Professor R. Titmuss), no. 19, 1967.

GAVRON, H. *The Captive Wife*, 1966.

HARVEY, E. Unstreaming a Junior School, in *Forum*, spring 1960.
HOLLINGSHEAD, A. B. *Elmtown's Youth*, 1949.

INCORPORATED ASSOCIATION OF ASSISTANT MASTERS IN SECONDARY SCHOOLS. *Teaching in Comprehensive Schools*, 1967.
INNER LONDON EDUCATION AUTHORITY. *Inner London Comprehensive Schools*, 1966.

JACKSON, B. *Streaming*, 1964.

JACKSON, B. and MARSDEN, D. *Education and the Working Class*, 1962.

JAMES, C. *Young Lives at Stake*.

LUNN, J. C. BARKER. Streaming in Junior Schools, in *New Research in Education*, Vol. I, no. 1.

MAUGER, P. Report of a Conference on Non Streaming, in *Forum*, spring 1960.

MAYS, J. B. *The Young Pretenders*, 1965.

MEAD, M. *Sex and Temperament in three Primitive Societies*, 1935.

MILL, J. S. *Utilitarianism*, 1863.

MILLER, T. W. G. *Values in the Comprehensive School*, 1961.

MORSE, M. *The Unattached*, 1965.

MUSGROVE, F. *The Family, Education and Society*, 1966.

NEWSOM COMMITTEE. *Half our Future*, 1963.

NEWSON, J. and E. *Infant Care in an Urban Community*, 1963.

PACKARD, V. *The Naked Society*, 1964.

PARTRIDGE, J. *Middle School*, 1966.

PATTINSON, W. Streaming in Schools, in *Educational Research*, June 1963.

PEDLEY, R. *The Comprehensive School*, 1963.

PLOWDEN COMMITTEE. *Children and their Primary Schools*, 1967.

PLOWDEN REPORT, Vol. II, App. 11, 1967.

RICHARDS, I. A. *Principles of Literary Criticism*, 1926.

SCHOFIELD, M. *The Sexual Behaviour of Young People*, 1965.

SCHOOLS COUNCIL. *Society and the Young School Leaver*, Schools Council Working Paper no. 11, 1967.

SCHOOLS COUNCIL. *Implications of Social and Economic Change*, Schools Council Working Paper, no. 12, 1967.

SCOTT, K. R. in Report of a Conference on Non Streaming, in *Forum*, spring 1960.

THOMPSON, D. Towards an Unstreamed Comprehensive School, in *Forum*, summer 1965.

WHITELEY, C. H. and W. M. *The Permissive Morality*, 1964.
WHYTE, W. *Organization Man*, 1957.

YOUNG, M. *Rise of the Meritocracy*, 1961.
YOUNG, M. and WILLMOTT, P. *Family and Kinship in East London*, 1957.

Index

adaptability, 7, 25
aesthetic education, 38–40, 43–50
aesthetic experience, versus entertainment, 40–45
  importance in life, 41–42, 48–49
Asiatics, cultural background, 90–92
  classroom problems, 92–96
Ayre, T. G., 80

Bernstein, B., 60 *n. 1*
Blake, Judith, 83
Bolam, R., 133
Brown, P., 133 *n. 4*
Brown, W. I., 140
Burgin, T. and Edson, P., 88, 93, 94 *n. 1*

career girls, 77
change, technical and social, 5–7
Clarke, H., 115 *n. 1*
competitiveness in school, 105, 121–3
comprehensive schools, 124–9, 130–1, 136–8
concentration, training in, 32–35
corporal punishment, 87–88, 167–8
craftsmanship, 26
cramming, 123
Crowther Report, 114
Curriculum Laboratory, Goldsmiths College, London, 28 *n. 1*, 138–9, 143

discrimination against the backward, 111
domestic responsibilities, training for, 75–76
Douglas, J. W. B., 101 *n. 1*, 112 *n. 2*, 114 *n. 1*, 116

eleven-plus, 112, 114, 117–18
entertainment, versus aesthetic experience, 40–45
examinations, role of, 146–7
  in literature, 47

family unit, nuclear, 19–20, 22
Farley, R., 167
Fitzherbert, Katrin, 79, 83–86, 90

Gavron, Hannah, 22 *n. 1*
Gould, Sir Ronald, 153, 154
group project work, 139–48
  assessment of, 145–7

Harvey, E., 129, 130 *n. 1*
Hollingshead, A. B., 128 *n. 1*
head teachers, 160–6
  lack of training of, 160–1
  selection of, 164
housing, 8–13
Hurst, A., 30 *n. 1*

imagination, 43–44
Imlah, Dr N., 12
immigrants, coloured, dispersal of, 97–98
  employment of, 99
  integration of, 97, 103
  See also Asiatics, West Indians
inference, practical, 27–29, 56
Interdisciplinary Enquiry. *See* group project work

Jackson, B., 115 *n. 2*, 116, 117
James, Charity, 142–6, 148
Jones, John, 141

Leith, G. O. M., 148

Lewis, Tom, 142 n. 1
literacy, 29–32
literature in schools, 45–47
Lunn, Joan C. Barker, 132 n. 1

Marsden, D., 117
maturity and immaturity, 48–49
Mauger, P., 133
Mead, Margaret, 78 n. 1
Mill, J. S., 40
Miller, T. W. G., 129, 131
mobility, 19
morality, as consideration for others, 51–53, 56–58
and utilitarianism, 54–58
and moral leaders, 58–60
Morris, Joyce, 32 n. 1
Morse, Mary, 1, 14, 15 n. 1, 24, 49 n. 1, 67
Musgrove, F., 2, 51, 113, 153

Newsom Report, 77
Newson, J. and E., 20 n. 1, 73 n. 1
noise, 15–16, 35
numeracy, 29–32

oracy, 60–62
overstimulation, 16–17

Packard, V., 14 n. 1
Partridge, J., 29–31, 111 n. 1, 113, 122, 150
Pattinson, W., 118, 129, 134
Pedley, R., 130
Pidgeon, D., 135
Plato, 40
Plowden Report, 31–32, 80, 87, 102–3, 107 n. 2, 109 n. 1, 115 n. 1, 131–2, 134 n. 1, 138, 157 n. 1
privacy, lack of, 13–15
programmed learning, 148

religious instruction, 62–65
research, educational, 107

Richards, I. A., 47
rootlessness, 19–23

Schofield, M., 1, 56 n. 1, 66 n. 2, 67–71
Scott, K. R., 133 n. 3
'second chance', 118–19
segregation, educational and social, 119–20, 128
selection, educational, 105–6, 109–110, 114–19, 136–7
setting, 124–5
sex, 66–72
sex education, 69–70
sixth form colleges, 60
Smith, L., 139, 140 n. 1, 141, 142 n. 1, 144
snobbery and art, 49–50
Sound of Music, The, 18
space, shortage of, 8–13
streaming and unstreaming, 113–114, 129–36, 156

teachers, classroom isolation of, 157
hardships of, 155–8
housing of, 155
influence of, 150
necessary qualities of, 151–2
promotion of, 155–7, 165
public image of, 153
shortage of, 152, 155
teamwork of, 145, 158–9
training of, 153, 166–7
as social workers, 160
television, as escapist outlet, 9–10
as an encroachment on lives, 23, 38
Third Session, 158–9
Thompson, D., 114, 118, 130

universities, 110
utilitarian approach, 54–58

vocational training, 25–26

West Indians, cultural background, 82–87
  classroom problems, 86–90
Whiteley, C. H. and W.M., 66
Whyte, W., 21 *n. 1*

working classes, 116–17
working wives, 72–75

Young, M., 19, 77, 83, 119